Brain Train
STUDYING FOR SUCCESS

● ● ● ● ●

Richard Palmer
*Tutor, The Open University
and Head of English, Bedford School*

and

Chris Pope
Student, Oxford University

E & FN SPON
An Imprint of Chapman & Hall
London · New York · Tokyo · Melbourne · Madras

**Published by E & FN Spon, an imprint of Chapman & Hall,
2–6 Boundary Row, London SE1 8HN**

Chapman & Hall, 2–6 Boundary Row, London SE1 8HN, UK

Chapman & Hall, 29 West 35th Street, New York NY10001, USA

Chapman & Hall Japan, Thomson Publishing Japan, Hirakawacho Nemoto Building, 7F, 1-7-11 Hirakawa-cho, Chiyoda-ku, Tokyo 102, Japan

Chapman & Hall Australia, Thomas Nelson Australia, 102 Dodds Street, South Melbourne, Victoria 3205, Australia

Chapman & Hall India, R. Seshadri, 32 Second Main Road, CIT East, Madras 600 035, India

First edition 1984
Reprinted 1985, 1992

© 1984 R. Palmer & C. Pope

Printed in Great Britain by St Edmundsbury Press Ltd, Bury St Edmunds, Suffolk

ISBN 0 419 13110 8

A catalogue record for this book is available from the British Library

Library of Congress Cataloging-in-Publication data

Palmer, Richard, 1947–
   Brain train.
   Bibliography: p.
   Includes index.
   1. Study, Method of.   2. Report writing.   3. Research.
4. Examinations—Study guides.   I. Pope, Christopher.
II. Title.
LB1049.P35   1984   371.3′028′12   84-10613
ISBN 0-419-13100-0
ISBN 0-419-13110-8 (pbk.)

Brain T

STUDYING F

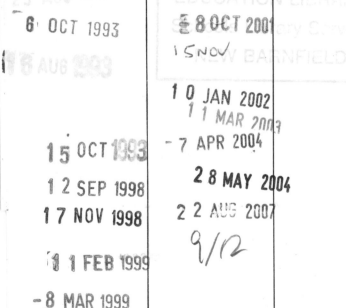

This book is dedicated to all my students,
past and present.

If it weren't for their enthusiasm,
interest and industry,
I'd have finished it in half the time.

● ● ● ● ●

Contents

• • • • •
Preface

No profit grows where is no pleasure ta'en;
In brief, sir, study what you most affect.
The Taming of the Shrew

This is a book about how to study; and its main stress is on enjoyment. You may find this combination surprising; if so, you're wrong. Study is like anything else: the more you enjoy it, the more you will succeed.

The book is written for the voluntary student – i.e. anyone over the age of sixteen. You've chosen to study, for whatever reason: to do well, you need to derive pleasure, even *fun*, from your work. It would be absurd to suggest that you don't need to work hard – of course you do. But there is no need for working hard to be a dull joyless grind which you resent and fear.

There are a number of books on study skills available now. Most of the ones I've read are sound and helpful, and some of them are more than just that. But nearly all of them, I think, are written in a dry and solemn way which can deflate the nervous student. In stressing enjoyment, therefore, I hope that you can approach your course with a feeling more positive than anxiety. It is highly improbable that you possess no talent: most students are a lot brighter than they think. Bear that in mind from the beginning, and you've taken the first important step towards regarding study as pleasure rather than as work.

I have, as you may have noticed from the cover, written this book in collaboration with someone else. Chris Pope is still a student himself: at the time of writing, he is about to go up to Oxford, having completed 'A' level in Maths, Physics and Music. He has written two chapters on his own; and elsewhere he has looked over and emended my own chapters. I mention this so that you'll know we're *on your side*. Much of the advice given to students, however well-meaning, experienced and sound, loses impact because the student is not convinced that the adviser 'really understands that it's like'. With a current student as my collaborator, I hope that you will not feel that way about this book.

We have divided the book into three sections. Part 2 deals with specific skills, while Part 3 is devoted to the thorny business of examinations. To begin with, however, we look at approaches to study, at how the mind and memory work, and at how you can find *your* best approach and method.

Note: Nowadays, at least 50% of students, if not more, are women. Notwithstanding this fact, I have throughout used the pronoun 'he' and its other grammatical forms in the everyday androgynous sense of 'he or she'. My apologies to any outraged feminists; but the alternatives are unwieldy and ugly.

● ● ● ● ●

Acknowledgements

Many people have helped me enormously with this book, not least my wife and family in tolerating my moods while writing it. I would like to thank Bernard Chibnall, late of Sussex University's Media Service Unit, whose courses for teachers first kindled my interest in Study Skills; and I am also most grateful to my good friends Guy Claxton, Andrew Husband, Tom Keeley, Tim Kirkup, Patsy Tennison and Derek Turner for their interest, advice and encouragement.

I am also indebted to John Penny for his illustrations; to David Kelly for his contribution on personal computers in Chapter 11; and to my collaborator, Chris Pope – not only for his own contribution, but also for his sensible and creative criticisms during the preparation of the manuscript.

Above all I am grateful to Chris Turk. It was he who first urged me to write this book, although he should not be blamed for any short-comings in it. He also sub-edited the text with tough but encouraging insight; and he wrote the chapter on Computers and Study for no more reward than a mere 'thank you'. It is a privilege to have such a kind and supremely able man as a friend, and a great fortune to enjoy his professional help.

Richard Palmer

PART 1

● ● ● ● ● ● ● ● ● ● ● ●

Approaches and attitudes – how to get the best out of your mind

● ● ● ● ● ● ● ● ● ● ● ●

1

• • • • •

Testing . . . testing

I like work; it fascinates me. I can sit down and look at it for hours.
Jerome K. Jerome

What would you say the following had in common?

(1) Getting up in the morning
(2) Writing an essay
(3) Cleaning the car
(4) Reading *War and Peace*
(5) Re-decorating a room
(6) Mowing the lawn
(7) Having to practise the piano
(8) Sending off thank-you letters
(9) Preparing a meal
(10) Chatting up someone you fancy

You might answer that, with the possible exception of (10), they are all unpleasant or a drag but will have to be tackled sooner or later. Another possible answer, though, is that they are all difficult to start doing, but that once you have started, they're not so bad – even pleasant. Initially, however, there must be a degree of motivation present for you to be willing to start the task.

Since this is a book about study, and since study, like all things, requires such initial motivation, it is appropriate to suggest that this might be paraphrased as your 'interest' or 'enjoyment'. Indeed, the emphasis throughout the book is on enjoyment. Few people succeed at anything while finding it dull; and most really successful people – whatever their job – derive an enormous amount of good old-fashioned fun from what they do. So just about the worst thing you can do when starting a new course is to dwell miserably on what hard work it's going to be. If you *expect* a course to be difficult, obscure or boring, the chances are it will be. From the start, therefore, cultivate a sense of enjoyment; believe in the pleasures and satisfactions that await you.

It is of course idle to pretend that any course of study does not involve work – hard work. But the key to that phrase lies in the adjective 'hard'. If you think it means 'laborious', or its cousin 'tedious', you're going to lose a lot of will power immediately. If, however, you can latch on to the alternative meaning, of 'muscular' or 'concentrated', you will be setting up a tough and clear-sighted attitude which will sponsor enjoyment. All success requires care and industry: if you've picked up this book hoping for some smart alec way to by-pass necessary toil, you might as well put it down again right away.

I am assuming from the start that you are past the age of intellectual consent. For my purpose that is the same as the law prescribes in more physical matters: sixteen. Up to that age, in the United Kingdom at least, school is compulsory, and you may not have any choice about how you study and what. After sixteen, it is up to you. You can stay on to do 'A' Levels, go beyond those to a degree or diploma course, or take up a course after years away from study. Since it is just stupid to go on doing something you really dislike, I further assume that you are more or less pleased to be doing the course you've chosen. If you're not, this book can I hope still help you. But some kind of motivation is necessary, even if it's only the pleasure of looking forward to when you stop!

To help you work out your own attitude in more detail, here are four caricatures of 'student types'. They are meant to amuse; but I can assure you that any teacher (and most students) will have encountered them all at some time.

The Would-Be Student

The WBS likes the *idea* of studying rather than the *fact*. Like the person who fantasizes about being a concert pianist, but never practises, the WBS enjoys the prospect of success, plans the way he will use it, but finds it extraordinarily irksome to get down to any work. He expects the teacher to do most of the work for him. Of course, he would be hurt, even angry, if it were put to him in quite this way. But it sums up his fundamental reliance on being served a regular diet of pre-digested information and opinion.

In schools this process is called 'spoon-feeding', and is regarded as a necessary evil. The authentic WBS goes further: he expects the teacher to pre-chew the stuff for him. Or, put another way: the WBS is a sponge. He finds remarkable any suggestion that he has to *think*, rather than merely *absorb*.

The Would-Be Student

The WBS is also hostile to exams, condemning them as unfair and evil. He constantly searches for tricks with which to out-smart the system. By the time the exam is imminent, he has bought his own body-weight in those dismal instant 'study aids' which now infest the market. Saddest of all, the WBS expends formidable energy finding excuses not to work. These are often brilliantly ingenious: one marvels at them, but also wonders what might have been achieved if their inventor had devoted the energy to doing the work.

The Earnest Student

ES is all mouth and notebooks. ES cannot for the life of him find anything in the classroom or at his desk remotely amusing: ES wants to Work, not take part in a comedy show, and anything as trivial as a joke wastes his time. ES doesn't approve of a light-hearted approach from the teacher; to ES, Teacher is God Almighty – until His fallibility is exposed. Then he becomes a liability, if not a menace. ES is a fascist, in the strict sense of that word: he expects Authority to be right, and right in a watertight fashion. ES doesn't like discussion or argument: they are either time-wasting or a fatal sign of ignorance and uncertainty. ES demands that everything be Relevant: all things not of direct and immediate benefit to his current studies are mere chaff. ES is also a towering snob, especially if engaged on an Arts course. Shakespeare is a Good Thing; stylish light fiction won't do at all. Beethoven Rules OK;

The Earnest Student

the Rolling Stones are noisy yobs, and as for Jazz . . . BBC-TV is properly serious; ITV is cheap and nasty. And if a passage has 'George Eliot' printed beneath it, it will be very fine; should the name 'Dick Francis' appear instead, it will be escapist rubbish. Naturally, no scrutiny of the text itself will be required.

ES may be able; or he may not. He may be vocal and aggressive; or he may sit in Olympian silence. Whatever his personality and talent, however, ES is absolutely clear about one thing, thank you very much: Study Is A Serious Business. There is no time for humour, digression, scepticism, tolerance of the non-serious, tolerance of most kinds, in fact. ES expects to end up knowing all the answers: he is not remotely interested in the questions.

The Lucky Student

At school, the LS is often known as a 'swot'. He finds it hard to understand why he attracts envy and hostility. He simply likes working. LS reads voraciously and enjoys lessons, even when they are apparently boring. Eventually the hostility ceases, even if the jealousy remains, for the LS is cheerful and at one with himself and his work, so that he disarms criticism.

LS does not always triumph. It's unlikely that such a natural worker will do badly very often, but he has his difficulties and failures like everyone else. Nor is LS necessarily 'gifted' or bright. LS will *become* brighter through his commitment to work: quantity changes quality.

His 'luck' is the luck of anyone fortunate enough to find an activity they love.

And if you *are* an LS, you don't need this book or any other kind of artificial aids: you've got quite enough advantages already!

The Admirable Student

AS is not a paragon. He gets fed up and bored with study sometimes, and has periods of total lethargy. But this is entirely normal, and he knows it and refuses to worry about it. Essentially, however, AS wants to learn, and is prepared to work at doing so. In no way should he be confused with the Earnest Student, who no matter how diligent expects to be *taught*. AS is unsolemn and open: he studies because he likes his subject.

AS accepts that what he is asked to read and listen to is worth taking seriously; but he is not unquestioningly reverent. If something jars on him, he will say so. AS prefers to be delighted and impressed, but his mind is not closed to the much under-rated pleasures of destructive criticism. AS is humorous, and finds laughter and even the occasional silliness an important ingredient of his enjoyment of study.

Most important of all, AS is humble. (This is not to be confused with modest.) He is neither afraid to be wrong nor determined to be serious all the time: he knows that the brain must have its periods of rest and moments of sheer laziness. AS does not worship his study at a shrine, but lives with it as an intimate pleasure. At best, he retains that quality of wonder that characterizes the child: he loves his subject, and particularly relishes the sense of his own progress and understanding. AS at his most impressive closely resembles Benjamin Franklin's ideal of 'the wise innocent'.

Well, which type are you? In fact, most students contrive to be all four types at different times: I know that *I* have. The obvious point to make is that the Would-Be Student and the Earnest Student are invariably unsuccessful students, while the Lucky and Admirable Students usually prevail with some distinction. And the single biggest difference between the two pairs is the ingredient I have termed 'fun'. The WBS, underneath whatever surface liveliness he may show, finds work boring and unsatisfying, while ES is so solemnly determined to improve himself that he forfeits all possibility of actual pleasure from the beginning. LS and AS, on the other hand, enjoy what they do. Underpinning all their industry, concentration, frustrations and disappointments, they believe that study, like life itself, is in the last analysis a pleasure.

By now you probably have a good idea of the kind of student you want to be. Attitude is very important, as is a degree of self-knowledge. But no matter how well motivated you are, no matter how temperamentally suited to the activity of study, there is always that difficult time when you've got to start. It's time to have a look at the launching pad.

2

● ● ● ● ●

Ignition

*A body continues in its state of rest or uniform motion unless
acted upon by a net external force.*

Isaac Newton

At the beginning of Chapter 1 I listed ten activities which I always
find difficult to begin. I also pointed out that, although they might be
difficult to *start* doing, once they're under way they're not so bad. Just
as a car requires more 'juice' to start it than keep it ticking over, so your
brain and body need more impetus to begin a task than to continue it.
Ignition in all things demands a lot of energy.

What I'm saying holds good for almost any activity, and there is a
good scientific reason for it:

That which is inert wishes to remain so.

That is a simplified paraphrase of Newton's first Law of Motion quoted
above. So is this next sentence, its natural converse:

That which is in motion will wish to remain so.

It's easy to prove the truth of these two principles. Imagine yourself
(body-weight between, say, 110–160 lb) straining to shift a boulder
weighing a quarter of a ton (560 lb), in order to get it rolling down a hill.
All your muscular effort will be expended on moving it the first few
millimetres. Once you've created even a tiny degree of motion, the task
becomes rapidly easier – until suddenly it will be quite impossible for
those same muscles to halt the movement.

The human brain does not operate in quite the same way; but the
brain, once started, worked awesomely fast. (Yes, even yours!) Indeed,
one way to ignite your study-energy is to remind yourself that you are
the proud possessor of the most powerful and sophisticated machine
that has yet appeared on earth: the human brain. Since it is so much

easier to start a task if you feel confident about it, I am going to dwell for a few minutes on some of the amazing properties of that small chunk of grey matter between your ears. I want to show that, no matter how dozy or stupid you may feel, your real capacity is staggering!

Your brain; or why you can look down on computers

The most sophisticated machine on earth: the brain

The human brain weighs between 2.5 and 3 lb, and is made of microscopic cells. The first mind-blowing fact is:

> **If it were possible to unwind the brain's tissue into one single strand, it would stretch from here to the Moon and back: it would, that is, be half a million miles long.**

I can't grasp figures like that, beyond the vague realization that they're sensational. Still less can I cope with the two overwhelming sets of figures that fill up page 11; but I can assure you that they are accurate, even if you, like me, find it impossible to imagine them.

Let's brood on those figures for a moment. 10^{100} (a convenient way of expressing Fig. 2.1(a)) denotes the number of atoms in our universe. When you consider that your little finger contains several *billion* atoms,

10 000 000 000 000 000 000 000 000 000 000 000 000 000 000

000 000 000 000 000 000 000 000 000 000 000 000 000 000

000 000 000 000 000 000

(a)

10 000 000 000 000 000 000 000 000 000 000 000 000 000

000 000 000 000 000 000 000 000 000 000 000 000 000 000

000 000 000 000 000 000 000 000 000 000 000 000 000 000

000 000 000 000 000 000 000 000 000 000 000 000 000 000

000 000 000 000 000 000 000 000 000 000 000 000 000 000

000 000 000 000 000 000 000 000 000 000 000 000 000 000

000 000 000 000 000 000 000 000 000 000 000 000 000 000

000 000 000 000 000 000 000 000 000 000 000 000 000 000

000 000 000 000 000 000 000 000 000 000 000 000 000 000

000 000 000 000 000 000 000 000 000 000 000 000 000 000

000 000 000 000 000 000 000 000 000 000 000 000 000 000

000 000 000 000 000 000 000 000 000 000 000 000 000 000

000 000 000 000 000 000 000 000 000 000 000 000 000 000

000 000 000 000 000 000 000 000 000 000 000 000 000 000

000 000 000 000 000 000 000 000 000 000 000 000 000 000

000 000 000 000 000 000 000 000 000 000 000 000 000 000

000 000 000 000 000 000 000 000 000 000 000 000 000 000

000 000 000 000 000 000 000 000 000 000 000 000 000 000

000 000 000 000 000 000 000 000 000 000 000 000 000 000

000 000

(b)

Fig. 2.1   (a) The number of atoms in our universe. (b) The number of interconnections one human brain can make.

you may get a vague sense of just how many 10^{100} is. And now you can gape a little more knowledgeably at the concept of 10^{800}, which is the similarly convenient way of expressing Fig. 2.1(b). As the caption says, that's the number of interconnections and patterns that it is possible for you to make, using the ten billion (10 000 000 000) individual neurons of your brain. As Tony Buzan says: 'your mind is better than you think'!* It is certainly far superior overall to the most advanced computer yet built, or even planned.

I am not the Luddite the last sentence suggests. Computers are electronic, and the speed of the electrical impulse is about 100 miles per second – not quite the speed of light (186 000 miles per second), but still quite nippy. Now, the majority of human brain functions are chemical rather than electrical, and such impulses travel significantly slower – about 190 mph (miles per *hour*). Sometimes brain-response *is* electrical. When a red-hot cinder flies towards your eye, or when a snake appears in your path, the primitive brain doesn't waste time asking the analytical mind what to do. It just does it, with the speed of instinct. Some sophisticated thought operates nearly as fast, especially when based on knowledge you are certain about and have used often. But human thought is mainly a chemical process, and significantly slower than a computer. That is the strength of a computer; but it is also its limitation. No computer can *think* in fashion comparable with humans. It can perform feats of seemingly limitless recall; in the time it takes humans to blink, it can warn, solve, illuminate and confirm. But it cannot think creatively; it has no imagination. A computer, whatever winsome and amusing anecdotes one sees in futuristic films, has no personality whatever. (If any of you have seen a poem written by a computer, you'll know what I mean.)

Compared with a computer, the human mind is wonderful. Not only do you possess a most extraordinary machine behind your face; you have also a unique personality fashioned out of countless experiences, influences, feelings, desires, and thoughts. Bring that personality in to work for you. I don't mean that you should be self-conscious in the obstructive sense, smugly watching yourself 'working hard'; nor do I wish to preclude that marvellous experience we refer to as being 'quite lost' in an activity that grips us. But if you stay sensibly tuned-in to your reactions, thoughts and condition as you study, you will work more efficiently – and enjoyably – as a result. Polonius, the interfering and tragi-comic character in *Hamlet*, may be a pompous ass, but his remark 'To thine own self be true' is a wise policy for any student.

Right: now you know how clever you are, and what phenomenal resources you have at your disposal, you ought to be feeling more confident about getting down to work. But, even if your mind is now

*Buzan, T. (1974) *Use Your Head*, BBC, London, p. 13.

willing, how can you get your body to agree? How do you get off the sofa, out of bed, or away from the television, and to your desk?

The pleasures of bribery

It is now generally accepted that most students respond better to the carrot than to the stick; and this principle is very well worth extending to your *own* treatment of yourself. If you approach your desk feeling sullen or resentful about working, you've lost the battle before you've begun. Instead, set yourself a prize or small indulgence that you can look forward to at the end of your study-period – a drink, a television programme you know you'll enjoy, anything you fancy. This makes the soundest sense, as well as being pleasant. Good work deserves some kind of reward, so get ready to spoil yourself in some small but merited fashion!

One study-aid that I've come across refers to this practice under the heading of 'self-contracting', which is an unfortunate phrase more reminiscent of a drastic method devised by Weightwatchers than any-thing to do with study. But the underlying idea is sound. It proposes a bargaining process between your various, and conflicting, desires. To cite Isaac Newton again:

For every action there is an equal and opposite reaction.

It's not simply pleasant to look forward to a rest and a treat: it's as natural (and important) as breathing. If you adopt this rhythm as a matter of course, you will enjoy your study much more, as well as making it much easier to *start*.

How *not* to bribe yourself

Self-bribery is no good at all unless you are tough about it. It is only useful if the reward is *postponed*: enjoying the treat first as a way of getting yourself into a working frame of mind is invariably unsuccess-ful. Putting something off, as we all do, is an insidious process: the longer we leave a task, the more difficult it becomes to get round to it. So on no account allow your bribes to degenerate into excuses.

We are all exceptionally good at finding excuses. It is an area where everyone is remarkably creative. And any serious student must be on his guard. If you really do feel ill or exhausted, then it is of course stupid to attempt any proper study. You need rest to fight whatever is ailing you; to put an extra burden on mind and body at such a time would be unproductive. But don't kid yourself that you're ill if you're merely sluggish or fed up: that feeling will often evaporate as soon as you start working.

Similarly – and this is more important if less obvious – don't believe anyone who suggests that it's not worth working for less than an hour. As I'll be showing in Chapter 3, the brain's optimum span of concentration is between twenty and thirty-five minutes; and it is surprising just how much can be achieved in that time. It also explains why virtually all school timetables have been organized around a lesson-length of thirty to forty minutes over the last hundred years. Such a period matches the brain's natural activity.

Finally: don't spend too long *organizing* the bribe! The treat you plan for yourself is a trigger – something to fire you into working. If you day-dream in too much detail about what you'll be doing afterwards, you'll lose the impetus and be back where you started – doing nothing.

Summary

You can, then, do a good deal to get yourself started. You can take comfort in the knowledge that *all* of us find it difficult to begin practically everything. You can cheer yourself up by remembering that your brain is an awesome instrument. You can increase your confidence even more by regarding your personality as a strength, as a powerful force that will help you to understand and master whatever it is you need to learn. And you can make all sorts of delightful deals with yourself to ensure that each time you work there beckons some pleasant indulgence to lighten your way. There are four good ways to bring a horse to water, or a student to his desk.

Mind you, the next step is entirely up to the horse or the student! Nobody can make you study – not even you yourself – unless you want to. Since, however, there's not much point in organizing yourself intelligently unless you *do* want to study, I will take it that it is now time to look in detail at how best to continue. You've reached the starting-blocks: how can you most efficiently plan the race?

3
● ● ● ● ●
Lift-off

We are wiser than we know.
Ralph Waldo Emerson

You have ignition. The brain has fired: its energy is compellingly available. It needs to be harnessed, however. What are you going to *do* with all this power? Where do you want to go? And what's the best way of getting there?

There are probably as many answers to those questions as there are students. But there are all sorts of ways in which you can help yourself to use that formidable energy sensibly and profitably. Here are a dozen 'tips' or rules of thumb, based on my own (and others') experience of being a student. If they have a common theme, it is that *you* usually know best what suits you, what's happening to you, what you need, and what you enjoy.

Discover your own best method of working

In schools especially, much rubbish is talked about the best working methods. Anyone who says to you, 'The way to work is this, and only this', or words to that effect, is a fool, and thus a dangerous guide. There are as many *ways* of working successfully as there are *people* who work successfully. If you feel you work best lying on a large cabinet-freezer listening to Cliff Richard while drinking Ribena-and-soda, I'd say you were pretty *odd*, but I wouldn't say you were 'wrong'. After all, nobody but you is *doing* the work: it follows that nobody but you is fully qualified to tell you *how* to go about it. So find your best method. Not your teacher's; not your friends'; *yours*. And stick to it for as long as it goes on succeeding.

Be honest with yourself, but not puritanical

Many students mistakenly imagine that working requires a Spartan environment and attitude. If such an ambience suits you, fine. But if it doesn't, there is no value in depriving yourself of pleasant working conditions simply because you feel it is 'right' to do so. Indeed, it is positively unwise to adopt such a practice. Part of you will be tense and resistant as a result, which will interfere with your concentration.

So, if you like working to music, then work to music, and tell everyone who nags you critically about it to do something difficult and dangerous with their hair shirt. If, on the other hand, it *is* a distraction, then stop conning yourself and turn it off. You might be interested to know that my father and I illustrate this principle of sticking to one's guns very clearly. He likes silence when working, as it suits his formidable powers of concentration. I, however, like to control my environment: I find silence a hopeless distraction and so use music to blot out external interference. We used to argue about this heatedly when I was at school: now we both realize that each way works for each of us. We're *both* 'right'; and we'd both be 'wrong' if we assumed our way to be the *only* way.

Similarly, if you are a smoker, and enjoy it (and what other reason can there possibly be?!), then smoke if it helps. A solemn determination to abstain from cigarettes is a good idea only if it helps you work. Any other reason is that of a phoney saint, and work requires enough concentrated effort without creating extra problems. Of course, smoking does carry a major health risk; but that is a separate issue from 'how to work'. The real point is that you should be comfortable and natural while working.

Identical considerations apply to any wish for a cup of coffee or a stronger drink: if you want one, have one. Obviously, it makes no sense to work in the condition sometimes referred to as 'tired and emotional'; but a judicious amount of alcohol may assist you. Alcohol relaxes the nervous system, and thus can increase your sense of well-being and enjoyment. As with all these things, the only criterion is your awareness of yourself: if even the slightest suspicion of booze in your system renders you mentally chaotic, then put that bottle down at once!

If you get bored with something, then STOP

The human brain is no fool. If it gets fed up, there's usually a good reason; and if it gets fed up during study, it's telling you it needs a change. Boredom is a *positive* message. Nobody performs well when bored – a fact that unites cooks, footballers, interior decorators, astronauts and gigolos. So if you feel suddenly bored, two possibilities suggest themselves: either it's the work's fault, or yours. If it is your fault, then *do* something about it – stop day-dreaming, start concentrating properly, and so on. If it's the work's fault, then shelve it, and find something else to do until you can return refreshed to the original task.

As I said on the very first page, there's no point in pretending that study does not involve hard work; and it is inevitable that at times your work will seem joyless and a mere grind. Any area of study, however fascinating and pleasurable in over-all terms, will include some dull parts. It is not dangerously exciting, for example, to learn those French verbs which take *être* in the perfect tense rather than *avoir*; but you can't write, or read, 'decent' French without knowing the rules. So it has to be learnt. Similarly, very few pianists faint with delight while playing scales; but without such creative discipline, they are lost, and will be incapable of interpreting Chopin, say, with beauty and authority, because they can't actually play the notes.

Given this, the only recourse is to wait until you're in shape to tackle those necessary tasks. Naturally, if we wait *too* long, everything evaporates; so a certain toughness will be needed. That is true of all disciplines, physical or mental: the secret is to do it when you're best fitted. It's also worth while trying to enjoy it – if not for its own sake, then as a foundation for the genuinely enjoyable things it will enable you to do.

Divide your work into manageable chunks

In the last decade, a lot of research has been done on the brain's ability to retain things. We now know that if you plot retention against time spent, it will look like Fig. 3.1. The horizontal axis covers two hours. Notice that retention is high for about half an hour, but declines steadily thereafter, and only rises again towards the end. (*NB* 'Retention' can be replaced by 'efficiency' in the case of essay-writing.)

Let's consider that evidence in terms of your study. When you embark upon a two-hour 'block' of work, you are fresh and keyed up. Such energy will last for quite a while; but after 30–40 minutes, you will probably start to feel restless and a little tired. If you grit your teeth and plough on, the feelings of restlessness and fatigue will increase during the next hour, reducing your concentration and intake. Towards the end of the second hour, however, realizing it will shortly be able to take a good rest, the brain is fired with new energy. Indeed, the extra 'juice' this supplies may well take you slightly beyond the two-hour mark, leaving you feeling rather pleased with yourself.

But you shouldn't be all *that* pleased. For over an hour – more than half your working period – you've been operating at a level of retention never higher than 40% and sometimes below 25%. That may not be a complete waste, but it's not very satisfactory. It is even less satisfactory when you realize that a good deal of that particular hour's work will have to be done again.

Educational research does however offer some *nice* surprises as well. The interesting, and most encouraging, thing about Fig. 3.1 is that *the curve is more or less constant whatever the span of the horizontal axis*. With that in mind, let's redesign your two-hour block.

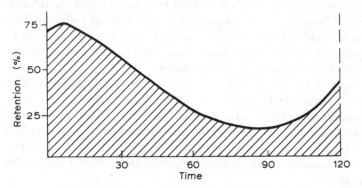

Fig. 3.1   How much the brain can retain in two hours.

Instead of working dutifully but not all that effectively for a single chunk of 120 minutes, why not divide the time into four chunks of 25–30 minutes, allowing yourself a 5-minute break in between? Your study-time can now be plotted in the way shown in Fig. 3.2. It doesn't require much thought to see that your total retention here is much higher than it was during the single two-hour chunk.

There is a further advantage to this method which the graphs do not show. By dividing your time, you give your sense of control over the material, and thus your confidence, a large boost. During the 5-minute break after each session, your mind will be 'ticking over' with a clear idea of what it's done and what it's learnt. Your mind will auto-matically review and sift its recent activity *without any conscious effort on your part*. When you restart, sensibly refreshed, there will be *added* energy for the next twenty-five-minute period.

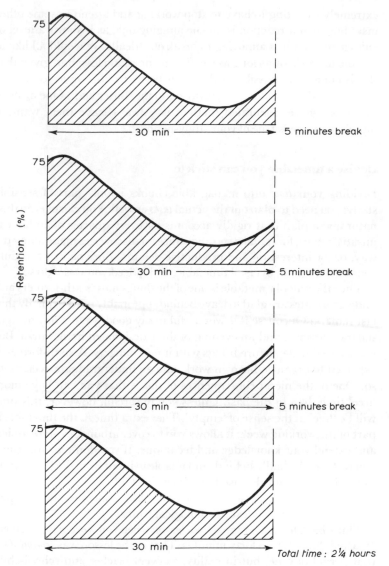

Fig. 3.2 How much the brain can retain after short breaks.

The graphs also demonstrate a point made at the end of the previous chapter – that it is *always* worth while to work for just half an hour. Although it is doubtless more convenient to have a longer chunk of time, it is not always possible; and it is certainly not *necessary*. It can be extremely irritating to have to stop working and attend to some other task; but such a reaction is an encouraging one, as it shows a level of enjoyment that it is annoying to break off. Ideally we would all like to be able to work for as long as we *like* – no more, no less; but, given that this is not always possible, I think it is better to stop while you're still enjoying it than to labour joylessly on to the 'bitter end'. One of show business's more celebrated mottoes is 'Always leave them wanting more': the same is true of your study-periods.

Devise a timetable you can stick to

Dividing your *time* into manageable chunks is only part of sensible study: you need to plan out the actual *tasks* as well. You can overdo this, naturally: a plan that rigidly accounts for every quarter of an hour is unsatisfactory, for it makes no allowance for discoveries made along the way, or for interesting and productive detours. But you can certainly construct a rough, over-all timetable; and indeed you *should* do so.

Since the school timetable is one of the things most sixth-formers and undergraduates are glad to leave behind, I probably need to justify that last remark! Of course it is wonderful to say goodbye to a day of eight separate lessons, and an evening of three designated homeworks. But this agreeable departure brings with it new dangers. A sixth-former is expected to organize his own work, and an undergraduate even more so. One of the nicest consequences of this is that you can have more 'free' time than in the past. Unless you're careful, however, this time will be 'free' in the sense of 'empty'. That extra time in the timetable is part of the working week: it allows you to cover ground, explore topics, and extend your knowledge and technique. If you don't *use* this time, you will soon be badly behind, and unable to profit from the lessons you *do* receive. So don't despise the school timetable as something that is now beneath you. Instead, cling on to its basic principles like a limpet: they embody the soundest psychological truths.

Think back to an average school lesson when you were, say, thirteen. It lasted thirty-five to forty minutes. That is, the lesson was *scheduled* for that period of time; but in reality, as every teacher and school-child knows, the first five minutes were spent getting everyone into place (including the teacher!) and generally settling down. Then work commenced. We will cheerfully assume that work continued at a fairly regular pace for most of the remaining time. It is likely, though, that the class (and possibly the teacher too) started to feel a little jaded at the twenty-five-minute mark, only to finish strongly as the prospect of the bell loomed nearer. Often lessons over-run because of this final 'up-swing' of energy. Moreover, children who ten minutes before were feeling the strain, or who had simply 'turned off', suddenly find all sorts of things to say and ask about as the teacher prepares to leave the room.

As you may have spotted, such a lesson-pattern is more or less identical to the pattern of the half-hour study-period described above (pp. 17–19). And that explains why the school timetable hasn't changed much, in terms of lesson-length, for a century. The span of thirty to forty minutes is the most effective and congenial for all concerned. It makes sense, therefore, to go on using the valuable principle of chopping up the day in the fashion you've now moved beyond. Work out what you've got to do over the next week, and divide it into chunks you can cope with. It's a good idea to write the tasks down and tick them off as you complete them, thus giving you an immediate record of achievement.

It is also important not to try to do too much, especially at first. I don't want to encourage laziness; but do make sure that the targets you set yourself are realistic. To take an absurd case: it would be insane to read Dickens's *Our Mutual Friend* (some 900 pages) in four hours. Less comic, but no less impossible, would be an attempt to master *absolutely* thirty pages of a closely argued textbook in the same time. You can certainly expect to acquire a healthy sense of the material, its main outlines and arguments; but it will be some time before all the material is there 'on tap' in your established, long-term memory. Total under-standing is never immediate.

You will find further information and advice on devising your own timetable in Chapter 5 on **Review**.

Keep physically alert as well as mentally aware

High on my list of people I'd like to reserve a cabin on the SS *Titanic* for are those posturing goons who talk of being 'in tune with your body', and extol the virtues of macro-biotic tomatoes and organically grown turnips. But a degree of intelligent physical awareness is important for any student. Thomas Aquinas once wrote:

Trust the authority of your senses.

It is excellent advice. We all have times when we feel stupid, sluggish or out-of-sorts. Equally, we can all be suddenly overcome with fatigue, when only ten minutes ago we were buzzing with energy. *Trust* these moments. Learn to recognize when to give yourself a much-needed kick, and also when to take necessary rest. There is no profit in either watching the day go by from the depths of an armchair, or in flogging yourself into some form of collapse; and your body will be aware of these states before your mind is.

Exercise is important too. The Romans coined a great truth when they defined health as *'Mens sane in corpore sano'* ('a healthy mind in a fit body'). If your muscles get slack and unused, eventually your mind will start to copy them. Nothing frantic or even athletic is required, whatever the notorious English Public School Code may say. But some kind of regular physical activity is an invaluable complement to intensive mental work. If you like playing squash, tennis, etc., well and good – provided it is safe for you to do so.* But if your ambitions are somewhat gentler, there are many small ways in which you can exercise. Walk to the corner shop rather than drive; run up the stairs two at a time instead of hobbling laboriously; clench and relax your muscles when stationary; you can even try sit-ups, toe-touching, and press-ups. (Appendix C lists some useful relaxation and everyday fitness exercises.)

Similarly, you can keep your *mind* in trim during non-study times with exercises that are also fun and relaxing. Crosswords are first class in this respect, as are all forms of puzzle and 'brain-teasers'. Reading a newspaper, listening to quiz shows, playing verbal games, and many other apparently light-hearted activities are equally useful as mental 'work-outs'.

Think of your brain as the strongest muscle you possess

This may be physiologically inaccurate, but it is an excellent metaphor. There are many parallels between the ways in which body and brain work. And there is no doubt that the mind and the muscles are alike in one central respect: they both work better when they're used regularly. When you begin a course, your mind will tire quickly. (This is especially true if, like many adult students, it is a considerable time since you last did any 'academic' work.) There is no need to be ashamed about this: on the contrary, recognize that the symptom is normal and healthy. Just as there are real medical dangers in pushing an unfit body too far, it is unwise to flog a tired and gasping brain. It's not dangerous in the same way, of course; but it's doubly useless, in that such a brain will achieve very little, and that will depress you and create feelings of

---

*If in any doubt about this, check with your doctor. I would not like to be accused of causing you cardiac arrest – especially in court.

inadequacy (which, given the circumstances, are unjustified). However, the more you work, the more active your mind will be, just as your body, as it gets fitter, will be able to take more and more pushing. As I've pointed out, it's awe-inspiring how much the brain can do; so, while sticking to my earlier advice to take rests when you require them, I can also promise you that a fit brain has a stamina and invention that you need never under-estimate.

Rest and recuperation

All work and no play doesn't just make Jack a dull boy: it will make him a lousy student too. If you cast your mind back to the Earnest Student I sketched in the first chapter, you will remember that one of his basic flaws was an inability to relax or to regard study as fun. Such a person attempts to be high-powered and solemnly committed *all the time*. This is neither necessary nor desirable. Nobody can be switched-on and continuously alert for sixteen hours of the day; so accept this as a comforting fact, and build rest into your programme.

We all have favourite ways of 'turning off'. My own is to watch junk television (of which there is a copious supply!). If you find yourself doing this for five hours a day, seven days a week, you are overdoing it! But everyone – especially those who spend a fair time each day concentrating fiercely on academic work – has the right and the need to be an idle moron for a small part of the day. It is of course up to you *what* you do. A delicious lazy soak in a bath may be just right; or a spot of gardening; or a gentle inconsequential stroll. Whatever it is, you'll know what best relaxes you and allows your brain to refresh itself for its next stint. You should both trust this knowledge and act on it.

One curious (but delightful) bonus of such a practice can be the sudden arrival of insights or solutions when you least expect them. The single most illuminating point in my own PhD thesis came to me while 'off-duty', half-asleep in the bath! And many of my friends and students have confirmed how often this kind of out-of-the-blue visitation can happen. You can get inspiration on top of a bus, in a supermarket queue, cleaning your shoes, etc., etc. The reason for this is clear: if you allow your brain proper rest and freedom, it will, even in its apparently idle moments, be sifting and considering the problems, and working for you unconsciously. There is, of course, a time to worry at a problem *deliberately*; but if you let the brain's automatic rhythms take over for a while, they may save you a lot of trouble, as well as allowing you to restore your energy.

Learn to be selfish

Oscar Wilde once diagnosed as a major ailment of our crowded and complex society, 'the sordid necessity of living for others.' Conversely, he also wisely suggested that the only immoral kind of selfishness was not that of doing as you want, but of expecting everyone else to live and act as you do. These ideas are worth exploring for a moment, for they are particularly relevant to anyone undertaking a course of study.

All human beings are selfish. What Freud termed The Pleasure Principle is basic to our nature: it is the desire to do what we want to do, and to avoid what we don't want to do. It is as silly to find this immoral as it is to call a cobra evil because it is venomous, or a shark wicked because it is a voracious and mindless feeder. All these things are fundamental to the creatures' make-up; and it makes about as much sense to feel *guilty* about being selfish as it would to blame the rain for being wet or the fire for being hot!

Study is a selfish activity. However supremely organized you and your family are, they are going to have to make adjustments and sacrifices in order for you to succeed. I am not suggesting that you adopt an attitude that is cavalier and insensitive, such as 'like it or lump it': that is Wilde's second point. But you will have less time for certain things that used to be a part of your life before you started the course; and it's silly to imagine that you can somehow expand your day to fit such things in *somewhere*. As well as the time consumed by your study, other circumstances or conditions will probably require adjustment. I said at the start of this chapter that it is essential to find your own best method of working and stick to it; and that means that you can't afford to consider everyone else's needs. If you need silence, find it. If you need space, locate some. I realize that this is extremely hard for, say, a home-based student with two small children, and I wouldn't dream of making light of such problems. Nevertheless if you simply decide to give in and 'make the best of a bad job', that is *exactly* what you'll do: a bad job. All good workers, like all good practitioners of anything, must finally be selfish. The number of people who have triumphed at an activity through sheer altruism can probably be counted on the fingers of one foot.

Never be afraid to ask

I am constantly surprised and touched by how anxious many of my students (both secondary and adult) seem to be about 'bothering' me with a question, or request for advice. They don't want to be a nuisance; they don't want to take up my 'valuable' time.

I'm sure I speak for every even half-way decent teacher when I say that being 'bothered' in this way is what we're paid for, and that it is also nearly always a pleasure. Naturally, a certain minimal tact *is* necessary. I wasn't all that polite, for instance, to a student who, following repeated absence at my classes, phoned me at *6.50 am* (not my favourite hour) to say that she was worried about her exams next day and could I help! Most of the time, however, teachers are only too glad to be of help to a keen student. Indeed, one of the qualities a successful student most needs is a willingness and ability to ask good questions: the resulting discussion stimulates teacher and student alike. So if you need help, ask for it. A teacher can do his job only if he knows what you know, and don't know: if you pretend or 'play possum', he will proceed under false assumptions.

The reason why many students *don't* ask is that they're afraid of looking stupid – if not to the teacher, then to their fellow-students. We've all known this feeling, and it is entirely understandable. All I can say is that, in over ten years as a teacher of both children and adults, *I've hardly ever been asked a really stupid question.* I've been asked questions I've only just answered; I've been asked questions that are irrelevant to the matter in hand; and I've been asked to spell out the obvious for nervy and anxious students. But at no time have I ever felt contempt for anyone brave enough to enquire about something they don't know or don't yet grasp; and very often the questions are so good that they open up a line of thought that I haven't previously considered. So don't be afraid to ask: it is only the student who *doesn't* ask when he needs to who is truly stupid.

(These remarks are developed at greater length in Chapter 10, **Teachers and how to use them: a teacher's view.**)

Keep reviewing your work

I discuss this fully in Chapter 5 on **Review**; but a few quick guidelines are in order now.

If you're reading, make sure you've understood it. Just scanning the words is no good: you must be aware of the structure of the material – i.e. where it starts from, where it's going, how it gets there. Academic reading is intensive: it will require two or three perusals before it is firmly fixed in the mind. Use this fact, and don't imagine you're 'slow' just because you don't pick something up first time. Re-reading will boost your confidence: you'll be able to feel yourself learning and growing.

If you're writing, regularly re-read what you've already done. That will keep your target in view, and also prevent flabby repetition. Also, re-read at the end as if you were an outsider – anyone but the writer. Read critically, looking for flaws and errors. I have no wish to turn you into either a masochist or a pedant; but the more mistakes or short-comings you can spot before the person who marks it, the better will be your work. You will also get a confidence-boost when you see how good most of it is!

You should always save ten minutes at the end of a period of study to mull over the work. This can be done as part of the 'winding down' process. The brain, glad to be resting, will be quite happy to run over the main points you've covered; and this will make your return to the work snappier and more fun.

Lastly, you should regularly look over your past work as the course gathers momentum. It doesn't take long: ten minutes a day is ample. There is a double benefit here, too: you'll recognize at once how much you've learned, and how far you're progressing. And when you come to revise at the end of the course, your past work will be familiar to you, so that you can *revise*, rather than having to do the work over again from scratch.

Remind yourself what your ultimate achievement will be

No matter how much you enjoy studying or how well you succeed, there are bound to be times when you get depressed or just fed up with it all. If such feelings occur *often* it may be time to ask yourself if you're doing the right course; but the occasional doubt and low moment are inevitable. So don't let these get you down: instead, just look forward to the time when it's over, and when you've got that certificate in your hand.

Sometimes, too, you'll find you get angry – at a low mark, or at someone's implied judgement that you're not as good as you need to be. Creative rage is a first-class study fuel, so use it. Whether your motive is to 'show them', or prove something to yourself, or (most likely) a mixture of the two, you'll find that some form of gutsy target-concentration is an enormous help. There's nothing like the prospect of the finishing tape to spur you on to greater effort, if only because you can have a well-earned, triumphant rest. And remember also that any worthwhile thing that any human has ever achieved took time, determination, and the fierce belief that it was worth it. It is, too; so keep that in mind.

Conclusion

A good deal of this chapter may strike you as being no more than applied common sense. I agree with you – except that very often that quality, apparently universal, and the only virtue that everybody is supposed to have, is highly *un*common amongst students. It *ought* to be obvious, for example, that *you* know best how you work, or that it's silly to go on working at something that has become catastrophically boring. But the fact remains that thousands of students pay no attention to these elementary truths, and go on working for too long in a fashion they've been told to think is 'right'.

Finally, let me say that I only want you to follow this chapter's advice if it's useful to you. If you *do* work well for three hours non-stop, then please accept my awed congratulations and pay no attention to my remarks about 'manageable chunks'. Remember, the two prime requirements for successful study are a sense of enjoyment and an honest sense of yourself. Nobody – least of all me – should bully or pressure you out of them. What this chapter has attempted to do is tell you about some phenomena I've noticed both as a student and as a teacher, and thereby assist you in getting properly into your work. The next chapter offers a detailed look at the student's most important, and also his most mysterious, piece of equipment: the Memory.

4

• • • •

Memory

O Memory! Thou fond deceiver!
Oliver Goldsmith

Goldsmith has a point: the memory *can* deceive, and often does. But we also deceive ourselves *about* our memory. How often have you heard, or indeed said, something like:

'You are lucky, having a good memory.'

or

'It's not fair: I can't remember half of what I need to.'

Luck has nothing to do with it. If your memory is poor, then it's not 'unfair': it's your fault. Happily, and more to the point, you can do something about it.

Of all the myths that surround Memory, the most damaging is that it is a *gift*. That is quite untrue. Memory is a *skill*; and like any skill its performance depends on application, on practice, and on regular training. Everyone potentially has a first-class memory; and everyone can train their memory, and thereby improve its efficiency.

Another fallacy that should be exploded here and now is the idea that there is a close connection between memory and intelligence. This myth is probably fuelled by the popularity of otherwise harmless and enjoyable programmes such as *Mastermind* and *Brain of Britain*, whose titles suggest that the ability to remember masses of unrelated facts denotes great intellectual prowess. In fact, all the research conducted so far indicates that memory and intelligence are separate faculties; and if you think about this for a moment, you'll see why. The difference can be clearly expressed by way of two definitions:

Memory: The ability to remember what you know.
Intelligence: The ability to work out what to do when you don't
              know what to do.

In short, memory is to do with recalling and using things you are *certain* of, while intelligence reveals itself most acutely when addressed to things you are *uncertain* of, or ignorant about.

Since your memory is part of *you*, however, some personal traits affect it. Your tastes and temperament will determine the *kinds* of thing you're likely to remember or forget. Some people find it easy to remember numbers but impossible to learn a language; for others, the reverse is true. But by and large the efficiency of your memory is a matter of training and taking care. If you *do* have a particular area where your memory is weak, then admit it, and work at it in the belief that it will get better. As I have stressed from the start, successful study involves being honest with yourself; and that applies to Memory as much as to anything else.

Short-term memory (STM) and long-term memory (LTM)

Memory comes in two types: the short-term memory and the long-term memory. STM is a sort of note-pad, which handles all the stuff we need to remember for a short time for immediate, imminent, or temporary use; LTM stores all the information we truly *know*. To put it in everyday terms: the STM is like a handbag or briefcase, while the LTM is more like a deep freeze, filled with 'no need to thaw' foods.

Short-term memory is like a
handbag: it contains
useful everyday things

Few sane people make a habit of inspecting handbags or briefcases; but picture one for a moment. If you're at all like me, the bag/case you have in mind is pretty full. Most of its contents are useful and needed; but some of them are useless, or rather have ceased to be useful. It's a rare handbag that does not contain a few screwed-up tissues or dead bus-tickets; equally, you would be pushed to find a briefcase that did not house the odd defunct letter or memo.

The STM is a remarkably similar mixture. Most of its load is useful and pertinent; but bits of irrelevant junk always seem to be floating around as well. When, say, you remember that you have to make a phone call at eleven o'clock, it's strange how that urgent reminder can immediately be followed by the fleeting recall of what you had for dinner last night, or how long it is since you washed your hair!

The reason for this is that the STM is neither organized nor fully in charge of its load. There is nothing surprising or amiss about that. Life is too short to organize *everything*; and most people lead the kind of busy lives that render it essential for them to carry in their minds an unrelated assortment of things. For day-to-day matters this is as it should be. I suppose one could devise a system whereby one could remember every single item required on a shopping trip without writing anything down; but why bother? The task, or the specific list, is a one-off thing; so it's better to save time, jettison the search for a

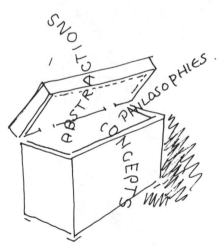

Long-term memory is like a
deep freeze : it stores information
for long periods

fool-proof mental stratagem, and simply write the items down on a piece of paper.

However, much of what we do describes a regular, long-term pattern, using information which does not change from day to day. Study is a particularly strong example – which is where the 'deep freeze' idea comes in.

An efficient deep freeze can store food for a long time. You can ignore its contents for months on end if you want to, and then raid it for something which can be cooked at once. The LTM operates in a very similar fashion. When you've *really* learnt something, it takes up a permanent residence in the mind, and is instantly available when you require it – even if you haven't needed the information for years. The LTM is, moreover, superbly supple, and elastic. It does not have to chuck something out in order to make room for new information, but simply stretches itself a little more. There is also a lot of evidence that suggests that the more you store in your LTM, the better it will work – just as a deep freeze works more efficiently if it is kept full.

It is, I think, obvious that successful study depends on the secure transfer of material from the STM to the LTM. It may make sense to make a shopping list for each trek to the supermarket; but it makes very little sense to have to look up, say, the date of the Norman Conquest every time you need to mention it. As your course progresses, you will be adding regularly to your store of knowledge, and to your growing mastery of the material. Indeed, it is usually essential that you do so. Most academic courses are linear: that is, you usually need to master point A before you can tackle point B, or understand concept C before you can progress to concept D. Since you are working under pressure, and teaching-time and study-time is restricted, efficient LTM-storage is a major priority for you. How best to do it?

As a way of answering this, try the little quiz that follows.

(1) Write down your name.   _____
(2) Write down your phone number.   _____
(3) Write down your car
     registration number   _____
(4) Write down your mother's
     maiden name.   _____
(5) Write down your post code.   _____

I would imagine that everyone reading this book had no trouble with the first two. I would also guess that, even if you managed (3) and (4) pretty quickly, they came to mind less automatically, and therefore rather *less* quickly, than (1) and (2). If you got (5), well done – I'd guess you are in a minority.

However many you got, the exercise is highly revealing. The ones you got right came quickly, if not at once. Those that didn't come quickly probably didn't come at all – unless you looked them up. It is a characteristic of the memory that it works very fast or not at all, as a general rule. If you have to 'rack your brains' for something, the chances are 10:1 against your finding it at the time.

But the real point of that quiz is this: whichever ones you got right, you did so *because you have been in frequent and regular contact with the information.* (5) is the best example of this truth: nobody but a rather odd pedant remembers their post code until they have *used* it several times on their own letters. After you've written it down a few times as an integral part of your address, it will stick: it will now be in your LTM.

If you apply the lessons of that little quiz to your study, you will see that the same principles apply. The more you keep in touch with information, the more likely you are to retain it. And this does not only apply to learning fresh material; it is just as important to revisit work regularly after it has been 'done'. First-time learning (which includes the writing of an essay) requires subsequent confirmation and back-up. Otherwise, no matter how secure the learning *seems* to be, and no matter how highly praised the essay, you will find that most of its information is gone within a week. It takes very little time to re-read your past written work, and not much more to mull over again reading you've recently completed; and that time is enormously valuable.

I extend this advice in the next chapter, **Review**. For those interested in a more detailed account of the short-term memory and the long-term memory, Peter Russell's *The Brain Book* (RKP, 1979) is notably good, being both comprehensive and very readable. (Chapters 6, 7 and 10 are especially useful.) But for now I want to move on to ways of accelerating and clarifying the process of memorizing.

Memory and do-it-yourself visual aids

As we've seen, the brain is an awesome and versatile instrument. And there is *never* a time when your brain is not doing several things at once. The phrase 'single-minded' may have a poetic truth in its suggestion of absolute concentration, but it is neurologically impossible.

Imagine yourself sitting in a chair, reading. You are deep in your book, concentrating fiercely: you are, apparently, absorbed in a *single activity*. Yet think of all the different things your brain is doing. As you read, you are aware only of the text itself; but the motor part of the brain is commanding your physical grasp on the book, the movements of your hand as you turn the pages, and probably several unconscious mannerisms. Various other stimuli and information are also being received as you read. The brain may be getting messages from all over your body, to the effect that you're hungry, feel like a cigarette, are shortly going to suffer cramp if you continue to sit on your leg, etc. No wonder concentrating seems so difficult!

Such a variety of simultaneous brain-activity could be most distracting. However, since there's no way of stopping your brain doing all these things, why not get the so-called distractions to work *for* you? For instance, all of us find that, as we read, a series of images flits across our mind. These may be connected to the material being read, or they may seem irrelevant. It doesn't matter; they are potentially valuable as spontaneous 'enforcers'. To take a ludicrous (but highly effective) example, let us imagine you are trying to learn, say, some chemical symbols. For no logical reason whatever, a picture of a very fat woman stuck in a revolving door suddenly flashes across your mind. Instead of *just* laughing, and using your mirth as an excuse to break off the learning-process, why not *fix* that image *consciously* alongside whatever symbol you were studying when it occurred. I guarantee that you'll remember the symbol very clearly, even if a few eyebrows are raised when you suddenly start giggling in the middle of a chemistry exam!

To make another, more homely example, I was unable for a long time (being essentially unpractical) to remember, when changing a plug, which one of the blue and brown wires was 'live'. I had to look it up or ask someone every time. One day it occurred to me that brown was the colour my hands would end up if I grasped a live wire; and I've never again had to think twice about which is which. A slightly grisly example, yes, but one where the image was directly relevant to what I was trying to learn. The principle is the same whatever the source of the image: provided you can find a way to link it to the material, it will strengthen and clarify your memory.

The beauty, and the fun, of this technique is that you do it yourself. Auto-suggestion is always powerful, because we are naturally very interested in ourselves; and any process which allows us to be self-indulgent while assisting us to do something worth while can't be bad!

Basically, any kind of picture or image will do, provided it is effective. The most likely to work, however, are images that are funny, obscene, dramatic or colourful. These four are strong because they reflect powerful and intrinsic human responses. (This principle is sometimes called the 'Von Restorff effect', after the distinguished psychologist's discoveries about the workings of the memory.) You do not have to work at or force your images. Indeed, you *shouldn't* do so: their strength lies precisely in their spontaneity, and their sudden appearance 'out of nowhere', beyond your conscious control. Once you start *willing* images to arrive, you've ruined the whole procedure, because you're now concentrating on the images rather than on the stuff you're studying. It's quite unnecessary to force them, anyway: just try keeping them away!

The importance of being unearnest

You may feel that these techniques are somewhat childish, and that 'games' of this sort are out of keeping with the serious business of study. If that *is* your reaction, I would first refer you to the portrait of the Earnest Student (see Chapter 1), and secondly point out that such games are not only useful but utterly natural.

Man, like most animals, is by nature a playful creature, especially when his play involves a degree of invention and creativity. Enormous advances in infant education have taken place over the last twenty years, mainly through psychologists' and teachers' recognition that the child's love of play is itself a form of learning, and that, sensibly harnessed, it can accelerate other forms of learning. In this respect, as in many others, we have much to learn from our own childhood. Wordsworth perhaps put it best when he wrote, 'The child is father to the man.' The patterns of activity we adopt when we are at our most inquisitive and our most natural (i.e. in early childhood) should be revered, not dismissed. Besides, games are *fun*; and the more fun you can derive from your study, the more successfully you will perform. It's worth reiterating, I think, that very few people have ever become masters of their craft by finding it boring and laborious.

Memory and environment: where were you then?

We have seen, then, how you can use apparently distracting brain-activity to work in your favour. But why stop there? Potential distractions abound *outside* your head as well as inside it; and these can be channelled in exactly the same way, so that they work *for* you and not against.

Let's imagine that you are sitting reading, and that you are satisfied with your immediate environment. That is to say, you've got silence if that's what you want, or some background music if you normally work that way, and that no obtrusive or irritating event is taking place elsewhere in the house (kids fighting, arrival of the fire brigade, someone efficiently hoovering in the next room, etc.). Even under such pleasant conditions, you're an unusual person if your eyes unfalteringly remain fixed on your book for a period of forty-five minutes. If you're at all like me, you will from time to time glance around the room, or look briefly out of the window. This is especially likely if you are *thinking* as you read (and you should be!). Sometimes, you'll need to consider a point raised by the text, or ponder the significance of the episode you've just read. You may even occasionally shut your eyes while repeating an important idea to yourself in order to fix it more firmly.

At these moments, the brain will be taking in data about its environment, even if your forebrain is not concentrating on such things. We speak of gazing 'unseeingly' at something while we're 'miles away' and not focusing; but in fact some neural trace of what the eyes rest on will remain in the memory. So try to take note of what you stare at when raising your eyes briefly from the book. Such a visual record will help you to recall the material you were reading at the time.

In this way, your fleeting glances act as memory-triggers. Provided there's an elementary sensory memory present, it should be possible to summon up the required intellectual record. For memory depends partly on environment: if, for example, exams were taken in the same room as the stuff was learnt, performance would on average be 10–15% better. So try to create a logical sequence of images, that attend a particular piece of information you need to remember.

Virtually anything can become a sensory aide-memoire or 'trigger'. One student of mine was an inveterate gum-chewer – not always a pretty sight, but useful to him as an aid to concentration. He found that chewing a particular flavour of gum was a remarkably effective trigger – no doubt because he had been chewing it (although let's hope it was a different *piece*!) when first learning the material. Taste, smell, touch; all can be mobilized if you can find a natural and convenient method of bringing them in.

Incidentally, it is in this respect that background music can be an advantage. Most of us find that records acquire, over a period of time, a mysterious extra dimension: the grooves not only preserve the actual music, but seem saturated with our memories. The most dramatic instances recall to us some powerful emotion – great joy, unhappiness, fear, or desire; but less intense experiences can also be re-created with remarkable force. I have several records which, when I play them, instantly and potently remind me of a certain time – a recall that includes who I was with, what time of day it was, and what the weather was like. Often, too, when trying to remember something I need to use in a forthcoming lesson or lecture, I find I can usually remember the music that was playing last time I perused the elusive item. To replay that piece is frequently the only trigger I need.

All stored knowledge is abstract in the precise sense of intangible: your brain is stuffed with valuable information, but you cannot *literally* 'put your finger' on any of it. So it makes very good sense to allow sensory and material things to assist and confirm that knowledge. Proust once declared that 'the past is hidden somewhere outside the realm of the intellect, in material objects which we do not suspect.' The past includes all that we have learnt; and the ability to relate material things to required learning can be invaluable. There is an almost unlimited number of ways in which you can do it. And as with so many things in study, *you* are the best judge. No matter that some private technique you evolve for remembering things would strike others as comic or even barmy: if it works, then stick with it.

Contemplative learning and intensive learning

No true learning is ever leisurely, because to learn anything requires you to focus and concentrate on it. (This is as true of practical and physical skills as it is of intellectual ones.) But there is an obvious difference *in kind* between the learning which

(1) Leads you to acquire a sound and sensitive understanding of a Shakespeare play
   and
(2) Characterizes the mastering of a list of German verbs.

The first type I have called *contemplative* learning. By that I mean that your knowledge results from your considered response as a total personality. It does not come from the mere absorption by your brain of the salient facts. This always has to be done, naturally: it's not much use having a sensitive response to *Hamlet* if you're also under the impression that he lives in Belgium and has a mother named Anastasia. On the other hand, you're never going to get very far as a student of literature (English or foreign) if all you do is memorize the text's external facts and as much of the text, word for word, as you can manage. No: contemplative learning depends on mature understanding and personal response. As it happens, this is hardly less true for physics and biology as it is for something apparently 'subjective' like literature. In this area, therefore, memory would seem to be less important than personality and experiencing.

Think about that for a moment, however. 'Personality and experience': what is that if it *isn't* memory? One of the saddest things about amnesiacs is that the loss of their memory causes their personality to disintegrate. Without recourse to stored personal memories, they are as vulnerable and ignorant as small children. They have no guidelines as to how they want to, or should, behave. They become as totally dependent on others as small children are, and even more helplessly 'paralysed' than a wheelchair victim.

So in fact memory *is* a vital part of contemplative learning, since in some sense you *are* your memory. So you should bring as much of yourself to bear on your studies as you can. You will have lived at least sixteen years: you have experienced literally millions of things. So *use* them. I do *not* mean you should reject as unreal everything you encounter in your studies that has not (yet) happened to you: that would be silly. Neither should you be excessively humble. If something jars on you as wrong or unconvincing (or just inadequate), then *explore* the reaction. You'll probably find that your dissatisfaction is rooted in something you remember observing, or feeling, or sensing. Such a memory or experience will not, of course, automatically mean that you're 'right'; but it will increase the quality of your thinking and arguing, because you're operating as a whole intelligence rather than as a disembodied brain.

Intensive learning is narrower and fiercer. The central point about it is that it depends on frequency and repetition. The first words you ever spoke were, almost certainly, words you'd heard on hundreds of occasions beforehand. A little later, when you first attended school, I'd bet that among the first things you remember learning were tables – a process that drives most kids into a frenzy of rage and/or boredom while it's going on. But you will probably also admit that when it was over and you had achieved mastery of all your tables, you:

(1) Were delighted.
(2) Recognized, if only indirectly, that it was due to the repetition that had so bored and infuriated you.
(3) Found that the knowledge was automatic from then on.

A little while ago my younger daughter was in the midst of a campaign of deep hatred against tables. Indeed, her comments featured a number of what I'll call 'unidentified flying adjectives' that are not normally associated with nine-year-old girls. At around the same time, however, the rest of the family noticed that she knew virtually every TV commercial jingle that appeared, *even though she despised most of them.* Obviously, such knowledge was the result of constant exposure to the various jingles: they had registered automatically (which is the whole idea). Despite initial resistance, we were able to use the 'saturation principle' to accelerate her mastery of tables. We would all, from time to time, fire random table-questions at her – 'four sevens; eight sixes; nine threes' and so on; and within a fortnight her campaign had dissolved. Automatic and unshakeable mastery of tables took its place.

This idea worked for two reasons. First, it made a principle out of the theory that some forms of learning have to be saturative; and second, we all made a *game* out of the process. Not much of one, maybe; but certainly more fun than sitting on her own, trying to do it by rote in a mood of boredom mixed with rage.

So, if you have to learn something intensively – i.e. commit it absolutely to memory – get other people to help you by 'testing' you at random and without warning. This semi-playful approach will rob the task of much of its immediate grind, and will also render your study more sociable. For certain things, you can even make a family game of working out mnemonics. (See pages 42–44.)

Memory and frequency

I've touched on this already, and more follows in the next chapter. One or two important points need to be made here and now, however. It is generally true that there is a direct link between recall and the number of times the specific thing has been studied or used. This was illustrated by the little quiz on page 31. But it is not *always* true; or rather, the link depends on circumstances at the time.

Let's imagine you've failed to remember something which, for one reason or another, you feel you *should* have remembered. There are three possible reasons why this has happened.

(1) You may simply not *care* enough about the item to have logged it firmly. (This is the subject of the next section.)

(2) You may not have looked at it or used it often enough for it to have stuck.

(3) You may have looked at it and used it thirty times or more, but

never with enough of your mind on it for it to be transferred from the STM to the LTM.

It is the third possibility that concerns me here.

We all have those tantalizing moments when the name of something or somebody eludes us, even though we've often heard it. At such times we say, 'the name's on the tip of my tongue'. This charming phrase is not altogether accurate, however.

There are two possible explanations for this phenomenon. One is that the information *is* stored in the LTM, but can only be partially or insufficiently retrieved. The reason for such a 'block' may be that the memory is being made to try too hard: as I've said, if you have to 'rack your brains' for something, it's unlikely to be produced at that moment. It's better to turn off, and let the information filter through naturally. Sometimes this will take a day or two; at others it may only be a matter of minutes. Of course, when you're under heavy pressure to remember something (as in an exam), it is difficult to relax in this way, if not almost impossible. But it's worth trying – if only because to worry at something in such circumstances is rarely successful in time.

That kind of experience is indeed analogous to having something 'on the tip of one's tongue'. But the second possible cause of such a block is not well summed up by the phrase. There are times when, no matter how frustrated we may feel in being so close to remembering something, we are in fact *nowhere near* to recalling it. We may say, when someone tells us the anwer, 'Oh, yes, of *course!*'; but we kid ourselves if we confuse such told familiarity with independent, fixed knowledge of our own. In such cases, the block occurs because we've never taken quite enough trouble to lodge the information securely in our LTM. Maybe, while more or less registering the information at the time, we've not been paying full attention to it. Or perhaps we've allowed it temporary residence in our STM, only to evict it a few hours later in place of something fresh. Or maybe it simply didn't seem to *matter* enough, and we thus allowed it slowly to fade away until it finally vanished.

Pieces of information like this resemble casual acquaintances. We may see them often, but they never become important to our lives. Indeed, they are hardly *noticeable*, and it makes no difference to us whether we see them or not. They may well be interesting and pleasant, and we may sometimes think we'd like to know them better; somehow, though, we never quite get round to it. Other people and other things seem more important: there just doesn't seem to be room for anything else. In the same way, certain kinds or bits of information may flit in and out of our STM half a dozen or more times, without ever becoming permanent. They don't strike us as important or significant enough, especially when something fresher arrives for us to consider.

We can extend the metaphor. Suppose one such casual acquaintance *does* become a friend. Then everything changes. That person *is* now important. As with all true friends, there is an intimacy and automatic confidence between you. It may be that months pass between your meetings; but you think of each other often, and when you do meet up again, rapport is instant and profound. The things we know and are confident about are just like close friends: we are sure of them, and are immediately and permanently at ease with them.

How, then, can you help your memory turn 'casual acquaintance' information into 'friendly' knowledge? Well, just think for a moment about the difference between those times when you're re-united with a close friend, and those occasions when you bump into someone you know slightly.

In the former case, you are (I imagine) warm, spontaneous and completely at ease, while the latter finds you slightly bemused and full of cliché. (I find I'm quite capable of saying such fatuous things as 'Oh, it's you' or 'I haven't seen you since the last time we met.') The crucial difference is *self-consciousness*, which is absent in the first case and sharply present in the second. My own feelings, when 'caught on the hop' in such a fashion, almost amount to schizophrenia – it's as if part of me has left my body and is watching me with contemputuous amusement, quietly advising me from time to time that it would be a great idea if I shut up.

If you transfer this kind of behaviour, notable for its prickly awareness of self, from the chance social meeting to the attempt to learn, you will see why some things refuse to lodge in your memory despite the number of times you've noted them. You have never truly *concentrated* on them: they've merely been part of a rag-bag of vague impressions. So if you want something to stick, you've first got to 'glue' your mind to it. Just staring at it time and again is not likely to be very efficient. It *can* work, but it's more probable that the information will skate across the surface and disappear. Writing it down is much better. For a start, more of your brain will be directly involved, because it will have to work your hand as well as absorb the visual material. Make sure, though, that you focus on what you write, otherwise the memory will vanish.

If you can, make a game out of the information. It's easier to remember a historical date if you can find a way to make the figure mean something else as well. Let's take the year of Charles II's ascent of the throne as an example – the Restoration of 1660. You might take '16' and link it with 'Sweet', and re-name '60' as 'Hour' (the number of minutes in an hour). You've now created your own puzzle code, 'sweet hour', which is easily remembered because you invented it and instantly decodable for the same reason. As with nearly all memory-aids, it doesn't matter what you use or how you use it: effectiveness, for you and you alone, is the only test. You are trying to work out some way of personalizing the information, of making it *yours*. For as soon as you've made it interesting, you will *want* to remember it. It's no longer a casual visitor, but someone you've invited in.

Perhaps the most obvious difference between friends and minor acquaintances is how much you *care* about each; and that brings me neatly to my text topic.

Memory and thoughtfulness: how much do you care?

Hands up all those who have never come out with a remark like this:

I'm sorry about your birthday card/my homework/that bill: I forgot.

Just as I thought: none of you! 'I forgot' is a classic social excuse, and we all use it at some time or another. In nine cases out of ten, it is accepted – mainly because we know we are all guilty of it. To be unforgiving and lordly about a particular instance seems hypocritical. The fact remains, nevertheless, that the excuse is nonsense; or, to put it another way, the words 'I forgot' are a kind of shorthand for

I couldn't be bothered/didn't care enough/was too lazy to remember.

I don't advise you to point this out too forcefully next time you hear it said: people can lose a lot of friends that way! But I *do* advise you to take it very much to heart in terms of your study and the efficient training of your memory.

If you have a normal brain, you are capable of retaining quite staggering amounts of information. To do this you must, however, *care* enough about each item to hold on to it. For the memory to house something, it has to matter to you: if you don't give a damn one way or another, your memory won't either. For don't forget: your memory is a *skill*, one of the brain's remarkable tools. It is not a mysterious entity given to you, and therefore somehow independent of you. It will be as good (or bad) as you care to make it.

I've stressed throughout this chapter the need to redesign information, so that it becomes more personal. (That's also why, incidentally, Chapter 3 included a section entitled 'Learn to be selfish'.) Such practice offers two interrelated benefits.

(1) The material becomes more accessible, more 'friendly', and therefore easier to care about.
(2) The very fact that you *are* thinking, and thinking creatively, is itself a way of deepening your response and understanding.

It is no accident that we speak of sensitive, caring people as 'thoughtful'. In precisely the same way, the more you think, the more you will come to care about the information you're studying, and the more likely you are to retain it as a result. It is also no accident that people who *do* have bad memories are rather dreary and aloof. They haven't cared enough about too many things, and thus they've little that interests them and even less to offer others.

Mnemonics: the value of do-it-yourself

This will be a short section. I'm not going to offer you a selection of existing mnemonics and mnemonic devices: if you're interested in these, consult the Bibliography at the end of the book, which will tell you which books offer detailed information on the topic.

The reason I'm not making such a list is not laziness, nor am I daunted by the competition! It is that I am far from convinced that many of the mnemonics that students are encouraged to use are of much help. Furthermore, they *add* to your workload rather than ease it. For example, Tony Buzan offers an attractive-looking number-rhyme memory system.* It is based on finding words which rhyme with the various numbers (bun/one, shoe/two, tree/three, and so on) and then linking the number-rhyme to the item to be remembered. The idea is soundly based – it makes use of the visual back-up principle I outlined earlier (see pages 34–36); and, as I say, it *looks* promising. But I have to say that no student of mine has found that it *works*. Or rather, the system works all right, but it *doesn't* save time. A lot of my students have found that the complex matching-and-linking procedure confuses rather than illuminates, and they prefer to learn in the orthodox, 'cold turkey' way.

* Buzan, *op. cit.*, pp. 61–65.

Mnemonics must be simple. Furthermore, they are far more likely to work if you devise them *yourself*. A successful mnemonic is a fine example of creative thinking; and quite apart from the benefit you will derive from an efficient memory-aid, you'll get pleasure from the fact that you invented it. Besides, in this area at least, it would seem that it's quicker to invent than to learn!

There is an excellent reason for this. Mnemonics are idiosyncratic things: most of them have a distinct character, which is an expression of the originator's personality. It's a matter of pure chance whether the personality of a ready-made mnemonic will match yours and, if it doesn't, you'll find it hard to grasp the mnemonic. Use your own talent, and devise mnemonics that you immediately understand.

Let me give you another example. At least 90% of my students find difficulty at some time or another in spelling the word 'necessary'. It takes a lot of them years to stop wondering whether it's two 'c's and one 's', or two of each, or one 'r' or two, or whatever. A pupil of mine once suggested that the class might use this mnemonic as an aid:

Never eat chips, eat sardine sandwiches and remain young

I thought this excellent, and very likely to work. But although it clearly helped some, there were others who went on writing 'neccesary', or 'neccesarry' and all the rest of it. They were neither lazy nor stupid: the mnemonic simply didn't register with them. When I advised them to devise their *own* sentences based on the same principle, it was much better. At any rate, they started to write 'necessary' correctly!

In the same way, some children find it easy and natural to remember the Green Cross Code in road safety, and why others find it only muddling (and thus potentially dangerous). Mnemonics are as individual as people. Sometimes a genuinely universal one is coined that touches a chord in all of us – e.g. the rhyme '**i before e, except after c**'.* But on the whole I suggest that mnemonics are best considered as a form of private game. Your own inventions will help you a good deal, and they're a lot of fun to make up, too.

It might, however, be useful for me to list again a few basic guidelines about the *kind* of technique that is most likely to work. So, remember that the brain will latch on to ideas most firmly if they are:

(1) Funny
(2) Obscene/vulgar
(3) Colourful

* Even this is flawed, though, for the different reason that it's not always *true* – as witness words like 'weird', 'deign' and 'height'!

(4) Dramatic
(5) Physical
(6) Logical. (It doesn't matter if the logic is clear only to *you*: after all, it's your mnemonic!)
(7) As bold or simple as you can keep it
(8) Connected with something that interests or attracts you

The more of these you can work in to your devisings, the stronger your mnemonics will be.

Memories are made of this

As a little bit of fun before we wind up this chapter, here is a form of memory test. In Fig. 4.1, page 46, there is a list of words. Get a piece of paper and a biro; and then, either read the words through to yourself, *once*, or get someone to read them to you at dictation speed. Do that NOW and then return to this page when you've finished. NB *Do not try to cheat! It's pointless anyway; and this is more of a game with educational connections than a test.*

Finished? Right:

(1) Write down as many words, *in their original order*, as you can.
(2) Write down any words that were repeated.
(3) Write down any words that were linked.
(4) Write down any other words you can remember.

It doesn't matter how you got on, really; but let me make a few guesses. I would imagine few of you got beyond four words in the correct original order, and none of you more than seven. (If you *did* get eight or more, write to me immediately!) You probably got most of the repeated words; and you also in all likelihood got the four Big Cats and most if not all the five numbers. As for the remainder, I'd bet that a lot of you got 'Julius Caesar', and a few other words.

As I say, your performance doesn't matter very much; the test is a playful examination of the principles I've outlined.

In question (1), you probably started well and finished well. This illustrates the learning curve on page 18, confirming that in most study periods or tasks, the brain retains more of each end than of the middle.

If you did reasonably well on question (2), that endorses the theory that the more often you encounter or use information, the more likely you are to remember it.

A similar principle to (2) lies behind (3). If you *connect* various items to each other, you stand a much-improved chance of retaining *all* of them, because of the connection.

In question (4) *random* selection is in charge. What you remembered depended more on your personality, your mood, and whatever private associations certain words may carry for you than on anything 'objective'. It has been suggested that anything incongruous or outstanding ('Julius Caesar' in this case) is usually remembered;* but in my experience this is not sufficiently frequent or consistent to merit special consideration. It would appear that *repetition* and *connection* are the truly reliable memory-enforcers, as Fig. 4.1 illustrates.

As a postscript, try out this test on your friends and family, and see how they get on. And if their performance is significantly at variance with what I've suggested, please write and tell me – I'd genuinely like to know. After all, experience is always more telling than theory: that's why educational research continues to be done!

Summary

The memory is perhaps the most extraordinary of all the many wonderful properties of your brain. If you want to pursue your knowledge of its make-up and function, then all the titles listed under 'Memory' in the Bibliography should interest and enlighten you. My own elementary survey has sought to provide a *foundation* of knowledge about its workings, based on the following principles:

(1) Your memory is *your* responsibility, nobody else's. It is entirely within your scope to improve it. If your memory is poor and remains poor, it's because you can't be bothered to make it any better.

(2) We all have a short-term memory and a long-term memory; and most study skills are designed to shift as much from the former to the latter as possible.

(3) The 'intellectual' or academic memory is not an isolated structure: the more images and prompts you can bring in from the sensory memory, the better.

(4) Memory-games, especially DIY mnemonics, are excellent aids. They are fun, and harness your personality to your memory, so that *all* of you is focussed on the business of recall.

* See, for example, Buzan *op. cit.*, pp. 49–51. The graph he includes on p. 51 demonstrates a 90% recall for incongruous/outstanding items. My tests, conducted with 500 pupils of all ages and both sexes, suggests a figure well below 50% is nearer the norm.

before	of
moving	have
have	solid
lion	leopard
shall	while
the	nine
motor	the
on	two
grass	jaguar
one	sleep
at	when
tiger	brave
the	four
Julius Caesar	of
case	room
three	

Fig. 4.1

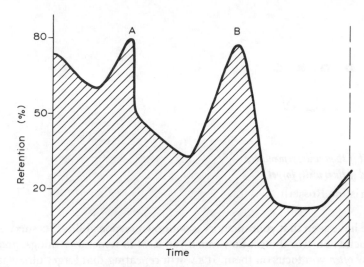

Fig. 4.2 How much the brain can retain. Notice the steady decline, as remarked on page 18, Fig. 3.1. Notice also, however, the sudden changes when the material has been repeated (A) and linked (B).

(5) If you want to remember things, you've got to *care* about them.
(6) There is something compellingly mysterious about memory. It has fascinated scholars for centuries, and there is still much we do not know about it. For your purposes as a student, though, it's best to adopt a sturdy, no-nonsense attitude to it. And as with any skill, a judicious mixture of hard work, play, and sheer *use* will make an enormous difference. If you sincerely want to remember things, it's remarkable what you can do.

The next chapter is closely related to this one. We've seen something of the memory's basic structure and behaviour; we have an idea of why we remember some things but forget others. Now it's time to see how we can keep knowledge fresh and available when we are adding each week to our total store of information.

5

● ● ● ● ●

Review

And if thou wilt, remember;
And if thou wilt, forget.
Christina Rossetti

We have seen that your memory is your own responsibility. Its success depends on two things: how much you *want* to remember things, and how *often* you focus on them. It's worth repeating that forgetfulness is rarely accidental. People forget things either because they have no real interest in them, or because they do not make *enough* effort to remember them. As Christina Rossetti suggests above, it's entirely up to you.

Let me dispose of one common fallacy. A 'photographic memory' is exceptionally rare. You may have seen espionage films in which Agent X or Counterspy Z has only to look briefly at a document, close and open his eyes like a camera shutter, and imprint the material permanently on his brain. Amusing; but reality is less easy. It takes work, not magic, to commit something to memory; and even when the information is securely lodged there, you still need to use it if it is not eventually to disappear.

Do not be put off, however, by this apparently forbidding piece of news. The 'work' required won't take much time, although adequate concentration is needed. Let me refer you back to the simple quiz in the last chapter (see page 31). We all remember our name, our address, our phone number, and a host of other personal details; and we remember them for a very basic reason – they concern ourselves. And all of us are naturally and deeply interested in ourselves.

But wait a moment: this needs a little more thought, doesn't it? Yes, all of us are interested in ourselves; but nobody but an idiot or a monster of egocentricity would claim that one's telephone number or post code are intrinsically *interesting*, even to oneself. So there must be an additional reason why they stick in our memory.

That reason is, of course, to do with the number of times we *use* such information. After we have answered the phone a bit, written down our post code or our car number a few times, we remember them automatically. But see how you get on with *this* quiz:

(1) Write down your National Insurance number _____

(2) Write down your banker's card number _____

(3) Write down your *previous* phone number _____

(4) Write down the name of your MP _____

(5) What was your timetable *last* year? _____

It's quite possible that you remember *some* of these without having to think for a while, or look them up; but I'd be vastly surprised if *all five* come automatically to mind. (1), (2) and (4) are important, certainly; but it's unlikely that you have to *quote* them very often; while (3) and (5) *were* important and frequently used, but are now defunct, and irrelevant.

'Well, so what?' you might be saying. 'What has my phone number of five years ago got to do with my current study and all the stuff I'm expected to remember at the end of my course?' Just this: that, if you want to log something in your LTM, the key to success is *frequency* even more than *interest*. You can be fascinated and moved by something you learn in week 2 of your course; but unless you look at it again, several times, in the weeks that follow, the chances are that by week 25 it will mean very little. The fact is that

The likelihood of remembering something is in direct proportion to the number of times it is studied.

Let us look at this closely, with the aid of some diagrams.

Now that you're studying for 'A'-level or an undergraduate course, it's unlikely that you have 'weekly tests'. You're doubtless glad to have left them behind; but they are worth discussing, because they illustrate a vital point about how your memory works.

Let's say it is Monday evening. Tomorrow you have a French test – verbs, nouns, and adjectives. There will be at least twenty questions based on about a hundred words you are supposed to have learnt in the last week. You work fiercely at that list, and by the end of the evening you feel reasonably confident. The next morning you have a quick consolidatory look, and, if you're lucky, another one five minutes before the test begins. The test is marked, and you get a good score. And on you go to the next section of work, which is a new list of things to be remembered.

Unfortunately, your French teacher is a sneaky devil. When next Tuesday arrives, he doesn't test *this* week's work, but the *previous* week's. Along with everybody else, you moan about how 'unfair' he is, and generally feel very hard done by. You feel even worse when you're told your score, which is now low. You cheer up somewhat when you find that the rest of the class has done equally badly, if not worse; and indeed you may have a good time afterwards, vying with your friends to produce the bitchiest phrase to sum up your teacher.

But your teacher may have done what he's done not to 'catch you out', but to prove a point. Let me demonstrate that point with the two simple graphs in Figs 5.1 and 5.2.

Fig. 5.1 shows the decline in your recall from Monday (x) to Tuesday (z) if you take no further look at the material you studied at point x.

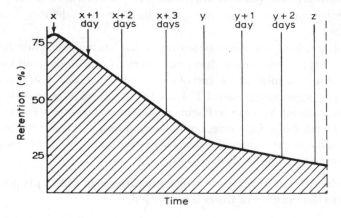

Fig. 5.1 Retention curve if work is studied at point x and not looked at again.

Note that recall is very high at the time you take the test (80%), but that by Thursday (y) it has halved (40%), and within a week (z) it is down to 20%, and continuing to decline.

Fig. 5.2 shows what a difference *intermediate* study makes. This graph shows the level of recall you should achieve if you look at the work again at points y and z. In each case, you restore your knowledge to its original level of 80% – quite an improvement on 40% and 20% respectively. Those figures are not exact – they will vary, according to your temperament, and to your natural ability in the subject studied. Whatever those circumstances, I can nevertheless promise you that such re-visits will consolidate and thus secure your knowledge much more reliably than if you leave it to chance, and only one perusal.

The nicest thing about this is that it will take you perhaps *ten minutes* each time you review – no more. All you are doing is to refresh your memory of things that were very recently learnt, and are thus readily familiar. Provided you concentrate properly for those few minutes, such review can be done at the end of an evening's work, or at any 'fallow' time. Indeed, such a practice is an ideal way of 'winding down' at the close of a work-session. The brain does not 'turn off' at once, and will welcome a gentle mulling-over of familiar material.

This principle can be extended to cover a period of months, not just a week. In fact, regular review throughout a course is probably the key to success. If you look regularly at your past work, your retention should

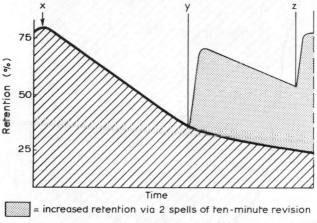

= increased retention via 2 spells of ten-minute revision

Fig. 5.2   Retention curve if work is studied at points x, y, z.

follow the pattern shown in Fig. 5.3. By the time you come to your sixth return to the material, it should be part of your long-term memory. In other words, you *really* know it, and it is as accessible and intimate a knowledge as all those personal details which automatically come to mind.

Feed-back

The principle of review becomes even more central when you consider that your work now includes more than elementary word-learning (and other such basic matters). You now need 'feed-back'.

Any advanced course (i.e. post-16) has areas which are less matters of *fact* than matters of *interpretation*. This is more obviously the case in subjects like Literature and History than in Science and Maths; but,

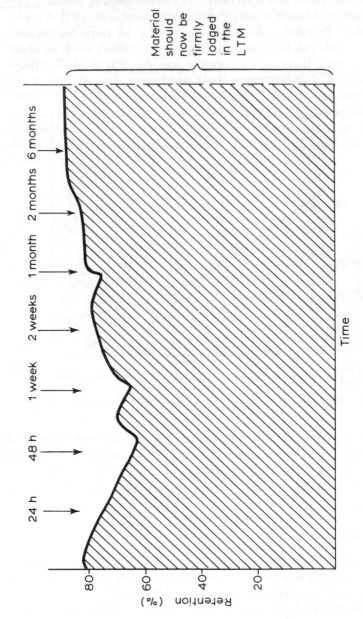

Fig. 5.3 The benefits of regular review.

whatever your subject, an advanced course requires you to *think* as well as *absorb information*. Or, to put it another way, in earlier years you could succeed by behaving like a diligent sponge, soaking up information as a passive receptor at the end of a *one-way process*. Now your relationship with both the material you study and the teacher guiding you should be a *dialogue*.

Later in this book there are two chapters on how to make the best use of teachers. At this stage I would simply like to say this:

Your teacher is not God, no matter how clever/expert/know-ledgeable he is or seems to be.

The sooner you stop being in awe of your teacher, and regard him instead as a wise guide, the better it will be for your study.

Since an example is more telling than any amount of generalizing, let us assume you have completed a long essay on the Causes of the Civil War (1642). Your next task is to consider Charles II's reign (1660–1685); so you start the preparatory reading, allowing the recent essay to recede.

In the meantime, the first essay is marked, and returned to you, with at least two or three comments in the margins and at the end, and probably considerably more. Some of these annotations will be criticisms or factual corrections; but the majority will be suggestions, talking points, questions, and ideas for your further consideration. Since, however, you are now fully engaged in other work on Charles II's reign, you may be tempted to do no more than glance at these remarks, concentrating on the mark and any actual mistakes you've made.

The *biggest* mistake you can make, however, is to do just that. If you don't *use* your teacher's comments, you are losing 50% of the value of doing that essay in the first place. For remember:

Actually *doing* a piece of work is only half the job; equally vital is what you do with it afterwards.

Unless your teacher is both lazy and indifferent, he will be only too pleased to discuss his suggestions and comments with you. But it is just as valuable to think them through on your own, using his ideas (and any new ones you may have had) as a springboard. Whether you discuss them with him or with yourself such a dialogue is essential. The practice has three distinct benefits.

(1) Reviewing recent work will help establish it more clearly in your mind, aiding eventual revision.

(2) Your *understanding* of what you've done, and the area of study it covers, will improve considerably. This will increase both the quality of your knowledge and your confidence.

(3) Your next task will benefit. Most aspects of a course are organically linked: to return to the example cited, a thorough understanding of the causes of the Civil War will almost certainly assist you in appraising the reign of the monarch who ruled less than twenty years after.

Courses are linear, minds are not

The human mind is a miraculous construct, but it is not always logical. Or rather, its logic, its patterns, and its connections do not follow a straightforward A to B to C . . . path. This enables us to achieve all kinds of things that are noble, exciting, beautiful, or witty; but it does occasionally make studying difficult, because most academic courses *do* describe an implacably logical, linear pattern. It is not my place here to debate the desirability of a system that places such stress on a particular *kind* of thinking at the expense of other kinds: rightly or wrongly, we operate in an academic world where student and teacher alike must adjust to the demands of a linear course. And regular review is one of the best ways of tailoring your mind to those demands. The more you become familiar with your past work, the better are your chances of grasping and enjoying present and future tasks. For regular review helps you to *build* a linear response within your mind, and thus gradually makes thinking easier, or at least more congenial. Your mind will continue also to work in its wonderful, non-linear ways; but you will have *added* a skill, even a dimension, to it, and thus made it even fitter for the job you have to do during the course.

Editing and adding

One of the benefits of a linear course is that you can see, fairly clearly, how much progress you're making. If you think of your course as a mountain (and many students do, initially at least!), then your months of study resemble climbing that mountain. At any point, you can look down and see how much you've covered, and look up at what remains to be done. Often, seeing what you've already achieved instils fresh energy and confidence to attack the remainder. The student who is in touch with his past work finds that a similar rhythm characterizes his study.

So it is both sensible and natural to use your present state of knowledge to edit or 'up-date' your past work. Review is not *merely* a question
of perusing your past work and 'learning' it: there is a more creative
side to the process. For instance, when looking back over past essays,
you may find it amusing to see what you wrote. Sometimes you will be
embarrassed by what you read, but this is a good experience, not a
humiliating one. Far more than suggesting how dumb you once were, it
shows how far you have come and how much better equipped you now
are. As well as this encouraging sense of your progress, there will be
things you've learnt and read since completing those early essays which
will alter your perceptions in a very concrete way. So go back over your
essays and annotate them *yourself*. This will deepen and freshen your
knowledge, and also sponsor the kind of friendly self-criticism that
toughens the mind – a quality necessary to every successful student.

Finally, a word about editing in the narrow sense of 'reduction'.
Early in your course, it makes complete sense to 'explore' topics in a
somewhat wordy or loosely structured fashion. Any *first* essay is like any
first reading: it will not be very efficient, there will be gaps in understanding, and style and structure may be awkward. This is both normal
and valuable. It allows you scope to develop your argument and your
understanding as the weeks and months go by. But when you *do* achieve
understanding, it's an excellent idea to go over your past work looking
for 'flab' – the sentences and paragraphs that don't really *say* anything,
but merely 'mark time' while you get ready to make your next point of
substance. Such a filtering process is not only stimulating in itself: it
will greatly assist you in developing exam technique, and it will make
final revision more agreeable. Which brings me to this chapter's final
section.

Taking the misery out of revision

For a great many students, 'revision' is a sad and terrifying misnomer.
Two weeks before the exam, they return to all the past year's work, and
make the appalling discovery that hardly any of it seems even remotely
familiar. Their 'revision' is, largely, not revision at all: they spend a
frenzied and enervating fortnight learning again *from scratch*. Perhaps
that's why so many examinees look so dreadful when they arrive at the
exam hall – pasty and drained, with bloodshot eyes and trembling
hands. It's hardly surprising: *anyone* would look awful after trying to do
six months' work in two weeks.

If you follow the advice in this chapter, you should never be in that position. When you come to revise, you'll find that most of your work is familiar, and you'll also find that the rest comes flooding back remarkably quickly. Of course, you may discover that you've changed your mind about some of the things you wrote earlier, or have since discovered new facts or angles that re-colour previous work. This is good: it means you are consolidating your knowledge in a healthy *critical* fashion that makes a clear and efficient exam performance much more likely.

Don't laugh; but revision should be *enjoyed*. It ought to be pleasant to dispense with classes to work on your own – however well you have got on with your teachers. If you've kept in regular touch with your work over the months, there shouldn't be any need for you to work while battling with anxiety. You can practise answering past exam questions (Chris Pope has some astute advice on this in a later chapter); you can test yourself or work with a friend; you can concoct little games that sharpen the memory and fully establish the major points you'll want to make in the exam; and you can also – and this is very important – find out *in your own time and with no external pressure* which areas of your syllabus you *like* most. Virtually all advanced exams allow you to choose which questions you do; and it is always wise to pick the topics that you find most congenial. This is as true for Maths and Physics as it is for English Literature or Politics: enthusiasm is a pleasing quality at all times, and no more so than in an exam paper.

Above all, do not attempt to work *all the time* during the revision period. If you've reviewed your work regularly, it's unnecessary to adopt such a miserable regime. It is better to have some fun and some rest as well as working. After all, the exams will make demands upon your physical and mental stamina as well as your knowledge. It makes no sense to arrive at the starting-blocks exhausted and fed up. Ben Jonson expressed this principle unimprovably:

'Ease and relaxation are profitable to all studies. The mind is like a bow, the stronger by being unbent.'

Summary

I stressed in the last chapter that there is nothing miraculous about an efficient memory. If you *want* to remember things, that is half the battle; the other half is taking regular and careful looks back at what you've done. This makes your perception of it wider and more detailed; and the sense of dialogue between the work and yourself transforms it from a distant and forbidding stranger to an easy acquaintance. Best of all, it shows you that your study is organically *yours*. It is something that grows and functions as part of you, not some external construct imposed upon you. In other words, it helps you to enjoy yourself more. And, finally: it doesn't take much time. Ten minutes a day is ample; and the benefits of such a brief effort are hard to exaggerate.

PART 2

● ● ● ● ● ● ● ● ● ● ●

Skills and techniques

● ● ● ● ● ● ● ● ● ● ●

So far in this book I have dealt with the fundamental aspects of study. The first five chapters have focussed on approach and basic fact: how the mind works, finding the right attitude and working method, trusting your own instincts, and so on. By concentrating on how to start, how to adopt a working rhythm that is natural and pleasant, and how to keep in touch with your past work, I have tried to give you a sense of the *over-all shape* of study. This feeling is essential to real efficiency and success. I hope by now you have an idea of how good your mind can be, and how much you are capable of. Above all, I hope I have convinced you that a sense of fun is not only possible but desirable: whatever your reasons for doing the course, you will do much better if you enjoy yourself. A proper sense of vanity is conducive to all successful study!

It is now time to look in detail at specific skills. The next chapters offer advice on techniques that are, unfortunately, rarely taught in schools or colleges. I would guess that few of you have received any systematic advice on how to take notes, how to plan essays, how to read quickly and efficiently, or even how best to prepare yourself for exams. But remember that, as with everything in this book, my ideas are *advice*, not *orders*. They are designed to help you, to give you something to think about and experiment with. They are *not* tablets of stone, so if you find that some of them don't work for you, don't worry: *use* that discovery, and find something else that does. Remember: *you are in charge.*

6

● ● ● ● ●

Eyes right: effective reading

Sir, do you read books through?
Samuel Johnson

Samuel Johnson devoted his life to books, learning, and words; so it is hardly likely that he intended the above remark to encourage mere dabbling in his own books or anyone else's. Quite the reverse: his incredulity was inspired by the knowledge that if a book is at all worth while, it will both need and stimulate several visits. The idea that anyone could possibly understand or fully appreciate a book just by starting at Point A and going through to Point Z provoked his most waspish amusement. We should all take a similar view, because

If a book's worth reading, it's worth reading twice; and if you want to get something substantial out of it, it *must* be read *at least* twice, and probably a lot more.

I am, of course, speaking here of 'serious' reading, not 'casual' reading for pleasure (although that too can be done more enjoyably once you understand a bit more about the nature of reading as an activity). The reading you do as part of your course is intensive and central – it is material you have deeply to absorb, and learn. And the notion that you can achieve such mastery at one go is clearly preposterous.

We need to be clear, however, *exactly* what is meant here by 'read'. So let us start by considering a few popular misconceptions about reading, and especially about what makes people 'slow readers'.

Misconceptions

'It is essential to read every word'
This is quite untrue. Moreover, it is a recipe for painfully inefficient and dispiriting progress.

Like a number of ideas that are both useless and damaging to advanced courses, this notion is a hangover from our primary school education. Please do not imagine I am casting scorn on those ideas *as such*: they are right for the people they serve – young children acquiring *completely new skills*. A child learning to read *must* focus fully on each individual word: how else can he build a vocabulary and acquire a functional sense of grammar?

But once you are into your teens, with a vocabulary that runs into five figures and a by-now automatic grasp of how sentences work, it makes no sense at all to abide by practices which are out-of-date for you. In the case of reading, this wouldn't matter if such methods were still useful; but they aren't. Consider, for example, this sentence:

The man in the wine-splattered raincoat tripped over the sleeping dog and crashed against the dustbins.

No word is unfamiliar, and no vocabulary-problem exists. It is not a *difficult* sentence: it describes two simple actions, and, though quite dramatic, makes no excessive demands on our imagination or our sense of logic.

But the person who 'reads every word' is going to find this sentence comparatively laborious: after all, it contains seventeen separate words. Most books average about four hundred words a page: you only have to think of such a person reading a thirty-page chunk of material to realize what a dreadful task any kind of extended serious reading will be for him. All those separate words – *tens of thousands* of them per half-hour session – not only slow him up appallingly, but also force him to work doubly hard reconstituting them into meaningful grammatical constructs.

You may be wondering what I'm talking about, especially if, like most of us, you've received no instruction in reading since the age of eight. A brief look at the way the eye works while reading will remove the fog, and demonstrate why 'reading every word' is a poor method. For the eye can take in more than one word at a time, and do so in a way that not only can make your reading *faster* but much more *efficient*.

'Fast reading is unnatural and bad for the eyes'

The human eye is an astonishing instrument; but it must *focus* in order to translate the image for the brain. To focus, it has to *come to rest* or *fix* on an object: it cannot track a moving object unless it is able to focus on each stage of movement. You can demonstrate this for yourself with a simple game.

Get a friend to focus on your index finger, which you should at first hold in front of his face at a comfortable distance. Then ask him to go on focusing on it as you move it slowly to one side and then the other; and *watch his eye-movement*. You can see that it is possible for him to 'track' your finger-movement only if he moves his eye at the same rate, constantly adjusting in order to maintain focus.

Words on a page are of course static; but, put together in the form of sentences and paragraphs, they occupy a breadth of space which requires the eye to move in order to absorb them all. The laws of its focusing powers, just described, mean that the eye must keep stopping, however briefly, to take in each separate static construct. But it has an extremely impressive *rate* of focusing. All human beings are capable of focusing on about *four things per second*.

In reading, this means that you can take in four words per second – *at worst*. At best, given a little thought and practice, this could mean twelve, eighteen, even twenty-four. In short, with nothing more gimmicky than alert concentration, you can increase your reading speed by between threefold and sixfold.

I'll show you *how* in a moment; but first, let's nail for ever the all too common belief that fast reading damages the eyes, which is as worthless as the related old-wives-drivel about the harmful ocular effect of watching too much television. (That may damage your *mind* with its plastic corn, but your eyes will be okay!) The eye is, finally, a muscle; and like all muscles, it·is the better for being used often and used efficiently. Speed-reading does not increase the *rate* of focus, whose optimum, as I've just shown, is four things per second. It can, however, greatly increase your *breadth* of focus; and that does not put any additional strain on the eyes at all. Indeed, because it makes reading more enjoyable and more satisfying, it could be said that it *reduces* eye-strain – if only because you can finish so much quicker, and thus give your eyes an earlier rest.

'Very fast reading-speeds are impossible'
It is said that the late President Kennedy could read state documents and official memoranda (items not noted for the elegance or easiness of their prose) at a speed of 1200 words per minute. Most people – including the author of a book on reading – have pooh-poohed this as impossible, and concluded that such a spurious claim was the invention of Kennedy's image-building team.

Well, 1200 wpm (words per minute) *is* a lot, I agree; but there is no reason to dismiss it as fantasy. I know several people whose reading-speed is at least 1000 wpm and many others who have trained themselves to go far beyond the 500 wpm mark that is popularly assumed to be the absolute 'ceiling'. How do they manage it?

Remember that sentence I gave you?

The man in the wine-splattered raincoat tripped over the sleeping dog and crashed against the dustbins.

Anyone determined to 'read every word' will, in effect, re-punctuate the sentence like this:

The . man . in . the . wine . splattered . raincoat . tripped . over . the . sleeping . dog . and . crashed . against . the . dustbins.

It looks ridiculous, doesn't it? But that's what you're doing if you focus separately on each individual word. Your method is, I regret to say, exactly the same as the toddler grappling with

The . cat . sat . on . the . mat.

Such a parallel is all the more humiliating when you remember that, unlike the toddler, you now possess a sophisticated sense of grammar. That is to say, you understand that sentences consist of words that build on each other, and make sense as *groups* or *sets*. That is all that grammar is, finally – nothing more (or less) than a system that enables and promotes clear understanding.

So why not *use* that built-in knowledge? Instead of reading every word as a separate entity, try to read them as *sets* of words. If you think about it for a moment, you will realize that they were *written* in that way. When we write, all of us think in 'blocks' of several words at a time. That's how I composed that sentence: you can see that it breaks up into three very easy, natural sets.

The-man-in-the-wine-splattered-raincoat
tripped-over-the-sleeping-dog
and-crashed-against-the-dustbins.

By reading the sentence in the way it was written, we have reduced it from *seventeen* separate foci to *three*. If you 'read every word', you will spend a minimum of five seconds on the sentence; reading it in 'blocks' shouldn't take you more than one second. In short, you've increased your speed fivefold at least.

Not only is this impressively faster: it is also more *intelligent*. As a consequence of reading *concepts* or *intelligible groups of words* rather than mere *isolated* nouns, verbs, adjectives and so on, you are immediately in tune with the writing's basic design and the logic of the writer's thoughts. Thus you will get the *point* of his writing so much more quickly. In addition to the increase in the speed with which you cover the text *spatially*, you are greatly accelerating your *understanding*.

To sum up: very fast reading-speeds are *not* impossible. You can do wonders to your own reading-speed once you learn to read in *sets*, a method that carries two huge advantages:

(1) You cover the print at – conservatively – *three times* the rate available to you in a 'reading every word' method.
(2) You double *that* speed by virtue of a much-improved *conceptual* grasp of the writing's direction.

So the claim that you can increase your reading-speed sixfold is not as optimistic as you might have thought. There will be times, of course, when the structure and vocabulary of the sentences you encounter will be a lot more complex than the example I have used, and this will inevitably slow your rate down. Even at its least successful, however, I can promise you that the method I've outlined will make a dramatic difference. There is no reason why you should ever be a 'slow reader' again. There is no need to 'read every word' in a non-literate, plodding fashion. Speedier reading is within *everybody's* capabilities; as an automatic corollary, so is speedier understanding. And for any casual reader, let alone the serious one, that is always the chief goal.

'Skip-reading is lazy and dishonest'

It depresses me how often I meet this attitude: it smacks of a sterile Puritanism, and also displays a basic ignorance of how people learn. Provided it's not the *only* method you adopt, and provided that you do not imagine that you can achieve *proper* understanding by it, 'skip-reading' is, sensibly employed, an extremely valuable method for any student, and particularly one who has a large 'reading load'. Its charm and effectiveness lie in its combination of offering a useful preliminary reconnaissance of new material, and supplying a welcome 'break' from the kind of concentration required during more 'orthodox' or severe reading activity.

'Skip-reading' is one of those apparently concise, but actually vague, phrases that can mean all things to all men. My use of it is fairly elastic, covering everything from a ten-minute flick through a 300-page volume to the more measured practice of ignoring the odd chapter. By 'skip-reading', in short, I mean any kind of coverage that departs from the A to Z, 'reading right through' method.

The value of skip-reading is that it allows you to acquaint yourself

Only a Puritan thinks skip-reading
is wrong

quickly with aspects of a book. Under no circumstances can it be considered as a *substitute* for 'full' reading; but it is a useful *accompaniment* to it. Best of all, perhaps, it has much to be said for it as a *preliminary*.

I've already stressed that any serious reading is going to have to be done at least twice. It makes sense, therefore, to make your first look at the material a brief and general one. If the volume/chapter/article has an introduction and/or interim summaries, read those first, as well as casting your eye over the rest of the material. This will help you establish from the outset a sense of what the stuff is *about*. In turn, that will help make your eventual 'full' reading more knowledgeable, and therefore more confident and alert.

Naturally, you don't *have* to do this. I find it works for me: perhaps it suits my temperament, or maybe it's just that I've always done it, and the habit is now an efficient one. If you don't *want* to skip-read, preferring to get the laboriousness out of the way early on, that's fine. It's no part of my intention to impose unsuitable or disagreeable techniques on you. But do not *despise* skip-reading, or, even worse, cultivate a sense of *guilt* or *moral disapproval* over it. It is no more shameful than it is useless; and if you find it helpful, then go ahead and do it.

'I'd like to read more, but I don't have the time'
This will be a very short section!

All I really want to do here is get you to see that such a remark is, in at least 95% of cases, pure drivel. Nearly all of us *always* have time to read more. If we don't, it's because we can't be bothered, or, more kindly, because we're too tired or sluggish to feel capable of taking on something as demanding as a book. This is normal and not in the least shameful; but it is an *excuse*, and as such should always be viewed with deep suspicion.

There are, it is true, some people who genuinely *can't* read as much or as often as they'd like to. The point is, though, that none of them is a student! Or, if they are, they must *do* something about such a time-problem. Any advanced course demands a lot of reading – be it Science, Humanities, or even practical courses such as Education Diplomas or Architecture. All the prospectuses I've ever read make this requirement absolutely clear from the start; and if a student finds that his 'reading-load' is getting difficult to cope with, there are only two possible reasons:*

Either: (1) He's reading unnaturally slowly.

Or: (2) He's doing too many other things.

Any attempt to put the blame for your non-reading on your 'impossibly busy life' really won't do. If you're advised to read things as 'back-up' material for your course and you don't do so, it's *your* fault. 'I haven't had the time' is a classic euphemism for *laziness*.

Very few teachers will give you a bad time if you trot out this stale explanation, because, frankly, they can't be bothered to chase you to do work you've *voluntarily* taken on. It's *your* problem, not theirs; and if you advance the absurd claim that you are so vitally occupied that you'd need a twenty-eight-hour day to accomplish all that you've been advised to, you can't expect more than a world-weary grin in response!

'Slow reading facilitates memory'
In a way I've already covered this in my look at the 'reading every word' syndrome. But the fallacy needs separate examination – partly because it seems so reasonable and wise that many can be seduced by it.

We've seen, in the chapter on memory, that the brain's natural (and therefore most efficient) span covers between twenty and thirty-five minutes. We have also seen that recall is usually instant or else not forthcoming at all. In view of this, it is hardly likely that a slow-moving attempt to commit things to memory is going to be more successful than one which is faster and more energetic. But we do not have to rely on such general logic: it can be demonstrated in a clear and concrete way.

* Discounting, that is, the possibility that you are doing quite the wrong course!

Find two pieces of writing, about the same length. They should, ideally, be pieces you haven't read before, although something you've vaguely looked at once will suffice. Preferably, your two pieces should either be about the same subject, or else about two subjects that you feel equally comfortable with (or equally uncomfortable!). If you like, two separate pages or sections of this book will do very well. Then:

(1) Read the first as slowly as is natural for you. Don't read it *more than once*; but don't go on to the next sentence until you're confident that you've understood the previous one.

(2) Take a few minutes' break.

(3) Now read the second piece *as fast as you can while retaining an intelligent sense of it.* Look it over again, *once* and *very quickly.*

(4) Take another few minutes' break.

(5) Finally, get a piece of paper and write down all you can remember about Passage 1, and then about Passage 2. (If you prefer, get a friend/member of your family to 'test' you on each passage.)

I will be very surprised if you find there is much difference between your two 'performances'. In fact, I won't be surprised if you've done slightly better on Passage 2 than Passage 1. Most of all, I'll be amazed if the five minutes you spent on Passage 1 results in you remembering *five times as much of it* as you do of Passage 2, which you read in a minute.

The fact is this:

On *any* first reading, your chances of digesting more than 40% are slim, regardless of the amount of time you spend on it.

If the material is at all stimulating, your mind needs some time and some room to come to terms with it. (This is one reason, incidentally, why a 'photographic memory' is an illusory concept.) You can *imagine* you've understood a sentence; but, by the time you've read three or four more sentences, it is likely that, although you retain an *impression* of that sentence that is enough to enable you to understand the subsequent ones, your 'absolute recall' of it will already be merely partial. You will, with slow methodical reading, acquire a sense of the over-all shape of the material, plus some individual points and ideas. But you can achieve *that* kind of grasp with the much faster method I've outlined; so why waste time and energy? You're going to have to read all your study-material again anyway, however slowly you cover it the first time: doesn't it seem sensible to deal with the first stage as efficiently (i.e. quickly) as you can?

I wouldn't be writing this book, let alone this chapter, if I were unsympathetic to 'slow' readers. What I *do* want to banish is the idea that there is anything *virtuous* or *automatically profitable* about slow reading. It is relatively easy to increase your reading-speed. What stops people from trying is that they feel both suspicious of fast reading, and cosily orthodox about the funereal rate they adopt. I hope the next section, which shows you how to read at considerable speed while *increasing* your understanding and retention of it, will convince you that slow reading is like a headache – not only does it have a clear cause, but it can be easily cured.

Speed-reading: a six-point programme

I ought to stress at once that this technique is not suitable for the reading of novels, or indeed any kind of 'creative' literature. Some advice about how to speed-read such works can be found in Appendix B.

That proviso aside, the programme outlined below will greatly increase your rate of reading, and is tailor-made for mastering text-books, discursive essays, articles, and most forms of course-work.

My 'six-point programme' means that you read the material in front of you six times, broken up in the following way:

(1) Read the headings, sub-headings, and (where appropriate) chapter-titles.
(2) Read the introduction, the conclusion, and any interim summaries there may be.
(3) Read/peruse any graphs, illustrations, diagrams, and tables.
(4) Read the *first* and *last* sentences of each paragraph.
(5) Fill in remaining gaps (= read it through in the 'normal', A–Z fashion).
(6) Review and clear problems.

Let's look at these six points in proper detail.

Points (1), (2) and (3) are self-explanatory. They are also very quick – which is very much the point. In, say, a concisely argued chapter of some thirty pages, it shouldn't take you more than *five minutes* to cover those first three instructions.

'Why bother?' you might ask. Well, those three rapid and highly selective glances at the material give you an immediate sense of the over-all shape and focus. They sketch out the terrain that you must later cover in detail. In this way, you acquire a grasp of the author's preoccupations, the direction of his argument, and the broad issues that he chooses to deal with. In short, the text is no longer alien, and you feel encouraged to dig deeper.

Many of us approach a book in some such way as it is. We read the blurbs on the back and on the inside covers, and we flick through the pages once or twice while we 'settle' ourselves. These three strands do no more (but also no less) than make a virtue and a system out of such behaviour, and make the initial reconnaissance less random and better focussed.

Point (4) is the oddest and the most controversial. Some students have rebelled at it at first, arguing that 'fiddling around' with paragraphs in such a fashion actually *wastes* time, and is an irritating distraction. This *can* be the case, I agree; but, much more often, I have found it enormously useful. For if you overcome its initial strangeness, the practice offers two benefits: it is a fine concentration exercise, and it also feeds you a great deal of information at considerable speed.

How? Get hold of a paragraph. (Any will do, provided it's adequately written.) Read it through in an 'orthodox' way. If the writer has any idea what he's doing, you will see that it follows a logical, even *predictable*, pattern. A paragraph, after all, is an argument in miniature: it introduces a topic, explores it, and then draws a conclusion. So one can assume that if one reads the beginning and end of such a paragraph, it should be possible to make at least an 'educated guess' at the content and direction of the material in between.

That's how the 'fourth strand' of the programme works. Provided you concentrate hard, and are not tempted to scan anything but those first and last sentences, your mind will *automatically* be drawing inferences and filling in the gaps for itself. So you can flit from paragraph to paragraph at high speed, while your brain estimates the likely nature of what you're missing out.

Of course, there will be times when those 'educated guesses' are inaccurate. At this stage of your reading, you are only getting to know the material, not mastering it; and it's inevitable that sometimes you will fail to take account of a point that appears in the middle. But even this is a help: the surprise you will feel at the subsequent discovery shows *how far you've progressed already*. For, even before arriving at point (5), where you read the text through 'normally', you are reading it *critically*. That is, you are reading with certain expectations, a sense of where the writer is going and the 'stops' he will be visiting along the way. Encountering an 'unscheduled' (= 'unguessed') stop will be beneficial either way: the writer's detour may be fruitful, or it may be unjustified. Whatever the case, your understanding of the material will have been considerably increased.

I should add, finally, that this technique cannot *always* be used – for the simple reason that some authors produce paragraphs that only have two sentences altogether! Such stinginess is not necessarily *bad* writing: I've seen several excellent science textbooks that use such a method to aid clarity. Usually, however, a good professional author will organize his paragraphs in a standard fashion; and that means you should be able to follow point (4) without undue trouble.

Point (5), as is outlined, restores you at last to the normal, A–Z method of reading. But there's a big difference from those times when you've adopted that method from the very start. Now you have a strong sense of what you're about to read. This not only means that you will cover the ground much faster; it also means that the various points and ideas will *register* much more definitely. An important by-product of this is that you will *enjoy* the 'full read' more. Your confidence will be higher because you know what the stuff's about, and you will also find it pleasant to have a *dialogue* with the text rather than have to plough submissively through it.

Point (6) is simply a kind of 'mopping-up operation'. It involves a quick look-over the material to ensure that you haven't missed anything important, or to clear up any remaining confusion.

Using this method, you will spend *less* time than you would on a once-through, A–Z, 'standard' read. You will still need to return to the material again at some stage; but you will have given yourself an efficient start that will make your reading more agreeable.

The other side of the coin: the pleasures and value of slowness

I have stressed speed a good deal in this book, and shall continue to do so. But that doesn't mean that I consider it to be a virtue *in and of itself*; nor does it imply that I think slowness is *always* a disadvantageous and inefficient quality. In emphasizing the benefits of speed, I have been chiefly concerned with two principles: one, that in many areas of study, quick and efficient work is invariably as useful as plodding, consciously 'solemn' study, and leaves you more time for other work and other things; and two, that it is quite false to believe, as many new or returning students tend to, that there is anything necessarily virtuous about taking a long time over a task. In short, I want to strip study of its Puritan implications, and to show that quick reading, quick thinking and quick writing are likely to make study much more fun, and more successful to boot.

But there are times when speed is not what you want or require. There is, for example, enormous pleasure to be had from slowly savouring something, and this is as true of reading as it is of more obviously physical pleasures like eating good food or sipping excellent wine. The six-point programme outlined above will, I am sure, help you to cope more enjoyably and commandingly with your reading-load; but there'll be times when you want almost to *luxuriate* in some-one's writing. This can apply to the science or maths student just as much as the arts one. I am a decidedly ignorant man when it comes to science; but I have always loved reading the precise and graceful prose of Descartes (who was a great mathematician before he thereby developed into a major philosopher) and the late Dr Bronowski; and I always take a long time over their work. This is partly because of my lack of talent in their subjects; but it's also because I *enjoy* the gentler rhythm with which their ideas work on me.

The whole point, in fact, about cultivating quick reading is that it then allows you more time for luxuriant, truly masterful and absorptive reading. From the start I've stressed that if a book's worth reading, it's worth reading twice or more; and sooner or later you will want, and need, to get fully and intricately into the book in question. Such a process can never be 'quick' in any real sense: indeed, there are many books which can take a lifetime fully to grasp and appreciate. (See Appendix B, where I talk of my experience with the endlessly rich novel *Anna Karenina*.) So it's not really, in the end, a question of 'slow reading *versus* speed-reading': it's not *either/or* but *both/and*. The sensible and alert student recognizes the value of both methods, and comes to know almost instinctively which one is most suitable for any given occasion.

Similar principles apply to slow writing. In the subsequent chapter on examinations, you will note that I don't have much patience with the argument that exams penalize slow writers, and that I argue that, by and large, good minds work fast when they have to, and minds that cannot do so are indifferent. I am convinced this is true; but that does not mean that there is *never* a time when slow, painstaking writing is valuable, and indeed superior.

Fast writing and thinking is the product of three things: healthy pressure, confidence, and command of the subject (all constituents of a sensibly set exam and a well-prepared examinee). But whoever you are, such a state takes time to acquire. It makes no sense to attempt a speedily efficient *performance* (which is, essentially, what an exam answer of any kind is) before you've reached a position of all-round competence following careful thought, gradual discovery, and clear marshalling of ideas. It is during this time that slow writing is both inevitable and valuable. This is the time when it *is* worth taking ten minutes to think of the right word, or a quarter of an hour polishing a sentence so that it is exact and authoritative; for, once you've settled happily on an idea or phrase, it will stick with you, and be instantly available when you *do* have to perform at speed. For the quality of a good mind working at speed (the mark of an expert, whatever his field) is *earned*, built up in stages and founded on the kind of committed care that will involve a slow and deliberate period somewhere along the line.

I develop these remarks on writing in Chapter 8. All I want to emphasize as a postscript to this section is that both speed and slowness are good servants but tyrannical masters. There is no virtue in being a slow reader, and indeed it becomes a vice if the reader is smug and lazy about it. Conversely, speed *as such* will degenerate into mere superficiality unless it is properly harnessed to a specific aim and technique. To be able to get the gist of a 1000-word article in two minutes is a valuable and beneficial skill; so is the profound and multi-layered understanding of a poem or a maths theorem, which cannot be achieved quickly. Both are vital and beautiful; and if I've stressed speed more than slowness during this chapter, that's only because, in my experience, far more students suffer from the problems of getting behind in their reading load than from the slap-dash, shallow appraisal that comes from inadequately devised or unwise quick-reading techniques.

Afterthoughts: speed-reading and prejudice

A great many people are suspicious of speed-reading theories: I was myself for quite a long time. My dislike sprang from those gimmicky and glib advertisements that still leer at us from newspapers – the kind of hard-sell that cannot long disguise the inadequacy of the techniques advocated. It wasn't until I read some sensible and honest work on the subject that I was persuaded that *anyone* can learn to read fast and efficiently; and as a summary I'd like to list the main reasons why.

(1) Surprisingly, moral prejudice has a lot to do with people's suspicions. They regard reading as a serious, even 'holy', activity; and they therefore resist the idea that it should be made easier. Such an attitude has a certain naïve charm; but it is finally just silly. If you

take books seriously, you surely want to get as much out of them as you can; and in view of that, to imagine that there is a 'correct' way of reading is no more sensible than to fancy that there is a 'correct' way of working. It's just you and the book: nobody else and nothing else count.

(2) Speed-reading is physically good for you, whatever old wives may say. The more vigorously and efficiently you use your eyes, the fitter they will be. Your eyes will get much more tired if they plod laboriously through a text that the brain finds opaque and joyless.

(3) The notion that speed and glibness are somehow synonymous is damaging and false. Ponderous people are rarely bright or interesting. Isn't it possible that their dull superficiality is the *result* of their slowness, rather than the paradox it seems?

(4) The brain and the memory work awesomely fast; and they also work best for comparatively short periods of time. The more you can do during that time, the more likely you are to retain it. Time and again, our experience shows that it is *not* necessarily the people who take the longest over a task who do it best, but those who approach it with energy, enjoyment and a brisk clarity of purpose.

(5) Serious reading of any kind is a gradual process, in the sense that full understanding can never be immediate. Speed-reading acknowledges this more sensibly than the narrowly dogged approach. Anything worth while requires several readings before it can be mastered: the decision to make most of them as rapid and pleasant as possible is not a dishonest short-cut but a properly intelligent way of bringing that moment forward.

(6) There is nothing virtuous about being a slow reader; more important, there is nothing *natural* about it either. Slow readers are slow because they lack sufficient understanding of how eye and brain work best, because they've been poorly trained, because they are imprisoned by certain silly myths, or a mixture of all three. If you *want* to read faster, you can; and I can promise you that you'll enjoy the activity more.

7

• • • • •

Creative doodling:
note-taking for fun and profit

Notes are often necessary, but they are necessary evils.
Samuel Johnson

Very few students, I find, have ever been given early, systematic advice on how to take notes. Some manage to develop a technique that is sound and helpful; but the majority are less fortunate. As a result, their approach to note-taking describes one of two equally unsatisfactory alternatives: the 'grudging' or the 'reverential'. See if you recognize yourself in either of these portraits.

The Grudging Note-Taker

This student regards note-taking as a pain. He'd go along with Johnson's remark, except that he thinks Johnson was far too tolerant in calling the practice 'necessary'. He buckles down to it eventually. But he neither enjoys it nor finds any value or stimulus in what is always and only a mechanical chore. His method and format are identical to the 'class-notes' his teacher dictates: they are cautiously and clearly spaced, written in formally correct English, and take a long joyless time to complete.

The Reverential Note-Taker

For him, note-taking is the magic elixir. He is convinced that all he has to do is write everything down, and it will through simple alchemy become fixed knowledge. His reverence is further demonstrated by his view of the printed word, and of the spoken word of his teachers: they are the academic equivalent of the Eucharist, profoundly present as

The Reverential and Grudging Note-Takers

soon as experienced, an automatic and immediate source of strength and wondrous new knowledge.

Such enthusiasm is so uncritical that it becomes self-cancelling. A 'normal' student who encounters a joke during his reading will laugh; the 'reverential' student will instead write '*Humour*' in the margin. Indeed, a colleague of mine once recounted an incident which shows just how far-gone such solemn mania can get:

'I went into the Lower Sixth this morning and said, "Hello." Three of them sneered at me, four of them said "Hello" back, and the other five wrote it down in case they missed anything.'

A slight exaggeration, no doubt; but most students, and nearly all teachers, will recognize its essential authenticity.

Both these types waste nearly all the time they devote to note-taking. One does it under protest, thus deriving little of value; while the other, by writing far too much and with no discrimination, ends up with at best a garbled and non-understood record of the book or the lesson. And both methods fail because no thought has gone into the vital question of *why* we take notes. It is that issue that I look at first.

The primary thing to make clear about note-taking is this:

All notes that are not accompanied by solid understanding are useless.

Unless you have a reasonable idea of what the stuff you're studying *means*, how can you possibly make useful, intelligible notes on it? (By 'intelligible' I simply mean something *you* will understand when you return to the notes in an hour/day/week.) And yet time after time students, at the start of a lecture, a lesson, or a TV programme, will at once launch themselves into a frenzy of scribbling – long before the focus or direction of the argument have been established.

Such a frantic approach is understandable up to a point, I admit. One's *aural* memory can be very short-lived, especially when listening to something as condensed as a lecture, and one is anxious to 'trap' the idea/fact/argument/whatever before it evaporates. Even so, it is much more sensible *just to listen for a while*, without the distraction of an attempt at simultaneous recording. In this way you can 'get into' the topic and so feel comfortable with it when you do start to take notes. All but the most abjectly bad lectures/classes/programmes will in some way 'ease' into their topic in a complementary fashion, announcing their main concerns in advance, and *repeating* each one as and when it is arrived at. So take in the main topics at the beginning, and write only when you reach them later.

The next point to be made is if anything even more important:

Notes are for *you*, nobody else. They are triggers and aids for *your* private use, and have no status whatsoever as public documents.

I stress this so forcefully because a lot of students imagine, when taking notes, that they must present them as if they were going to be *marked*. That is ridiculous. *Your* notes should not in any way be confused with the *class* notes your teacher dictates. *Your* notes are both part of your thinking and a reflection of it, done as part of the preparation for a piece of work, or as a record and reminder of your reading and research. They are nobody's business but yours, and nobody else should be in your mind when you make them. *Class* notes, though of course valuable, are quite different. The result of months or years of study and teaching, they are as formal as the textbooks you study, and a significant part of your course-material. This means, among other things, that if you want to make your own *private* notes on them, you should feel encouraged to do so – it is an excellent idea.

Methods

The taking of rough notes is as individual a matter as any other working method, and, as always, the only criterion is whether the method is successful. You will recall what I said about working to music, and the many other 'distractions' which students often feel they must deny themselves while working (see page 16).* The same is true of note-taking. There is no '*right*' way, other than what works for you.

So do your notes *in any way you like*. If it helps you to do them in alternate green and purple biro, *do* them like that; if you like weaving patterns or funny shapes with them, go ahead; and if it helps and amuses you to do them in a kind of secret code that you can understand easily, that's fine too. The more you can make taking notes a natural and pleasurable exercise, the more vigorously they will assist your study. That's why this chapter is called 'Creative Doodling': if you can make note-taking as automatic and 'un-work-like' as the doodles you do when on the phone or listening in class, you'll soon find that you are adding to your knowledge and skills while remaining relaxed and all-but-unaware of 'working'.

For anyone still unsure about what other methods *can* be adopted in lieu of formal, 'public' notes, and for the 'grudging' and 'reverential' type in particular, I now look at some specific techniques.

Key words

Introduction

It is a useful metaphor to consider a book, or even a chapter, as a living body. Its basic structure is analogous to a skeleton, and its major points to the most vital organs. Other things, which give the work its distinctiveness, are like the flesh and the idiosyncratic 'bits' which make us different from each other.

'Key word noting' is best explained with this metaphor in mind. It aims to isolate the skeleton and the major organs of an argument/episode, by focusing on those words or phrases that are clearly central. And I do mean 'clearly'. With a little practice, it ought to be fairly easy for you to register the main drift of a piece of writing, and to see which words/concepts are the vital ones. The added strength of this technique is that it should also be *very fast* – not only saving you time but giving you early access to the material and so boosting your confidence.

Let us look at an example. I would imagine that virtually everyone, be they Pagan, Moonie or Methodist, knows Christ's parable of the

---

* Now might be a good time to reveal that most of this book was written to the strains of Oscar Peterson, Stan Getz, Duke Ellington, and other jazz musicians. They relax and inspire me: what better mood could there be in which to work?!

Sower. With that story in mind, take a good look at the brief list beneath:

Seed

thorns

birds

rocks

soil

Sower/God

Those seven words form a skeleton of the parable. They should be all you need to put together a comprehensive version of the story and its allegorical meaning.

If, however, you'd feel a little easier with a skeleton that has been fleshed-out somewhat, you could add to it as follows:

thorns: the seed chokes/the Word is snared

birds: the seed is devoured/the Word is stolen (by Satan), and thus transformed and lost

rocks: no depth for the roots/the Word doesn't 'sink in'

soil: the seed takes hold/the Word is fruitfully absorbed

Sower: spreads the seed/God: spreads the word

All the other details can be recalled if you have either of the above lists as your base. The only other thing you need to produce an authoritative paraphrase of the tale is the ability to write adequate sentences. Incidentally, the listing of key words in this way is also an admirable method for essay-planning, as we'll see in the next chapter.

That first example was an easy one, because the story is so familiar. But the *principle* holds good for more complex, less comfortable material. I am now going to give you three distinct paragraphs, whose gist I think you can pick up remarkably quickly, using the 'key word' method outlined.

Practice and development

Paragraph 1
Here is George Orwell writing about the recent (1946) decline in the use of the English language. Pick out the 'key words' – write them down, or just ring them on this page. You should not have to read the

passage more than twice, and the exercise should take *three minutes at the most*.

It is clear that the decline of a language must ultimately have political and economic causes: it is not due simply to the bad influence of this or that individual writer. But an effect can become a cause, reinforcing the original cause. A man may take to drink because he feels himself to be a failure, and then fail more completely because he drinks. It is rather the same thing that is happening to the English language. It becomes ugly and slovenly because our thoughts are foolish; but the slovenliness of our language makes it easier for us to have foolish thoughts. The point is that the process is reversible. Modern English is full of bad habits which spread by imitation, and which can be avoided if one is willing to take the necessary trouble. If one gets rid of these habits one can think more clearly, and to think more clearly is a necessary tfirst step towards political regeneration.

Adapted from *Politics and the English Language**

The secret of the 'key word' method is *not to have too many*. This can be quite tricky to stick to, for if the writing is good, the prose will be muscular, wasting few words in 'flab'. That means that many words will be doing a fair bit of work, which can make the task of deciding on their immediate relative importance quite hard. Anyway, here's my list – see how it compares with yours:

> decline
> language
> political-and-economic causes
> slovenliness
> foolish thoughts
> habits
> imitation
> reversible
> think clearly

There are just nine concepts here, involving fourteen words. Plenty of Orwell's argument is absent, including the excellent analogy of the man who drinks. But if those words were underlined, ringed, or written down as I have done, they would form a pretty sound skeleton of the

---

* Collected in *Inside The Whale*, Penguin Books, pp. 143–157.

passage. Put another way, they provide nine reliable 'triggers' that soon detonate understanding and retention of the passage as a whole.

Paragraph 2

This passage is harder, I think – mainly because the author defines his central concern, 'totalitarianism', in a way that is far removed from our normal understanding of the word. So be on your guard; and remember that at this stage it doesn't matter whether you agree with him or not – just try to get the shape of his argument. Again, read it through twice, quite quickly, and choose the 'key words' or key *concepts*.

Totalitarianism has slipped into America with no specific political face. There are liberals who are totalitarian, and conservatives, radicals, rightists, fanatics, hordes of the well-adjusted. Totalitarianism has come to America with no concentration camps and no need for them, no political parties and no desire for new parties, no, totalitarianism has slipped into the body cells and psyche of each of us. It has been transported, modified, codified, and inserted into each one of us by way of the popular arts, the social crafts, the political crafts, and the corporate techniques. It resides in the taste of frozen food, the odour of tranquilisers, the planned obsolescence of automobiles, the lack of workmanship in the mass; it is heard in the jargon of educators; it lives in the boredom of a good mind, in the sexual excess of lovers who love each other into apathy. And it proliferates in that new architecture that rests like an incubus upon the American landscape. . . The essence of totalitarianism is that it beheads. It beheads individuality, variety, dissent, romantic faith, it blinds vision, deadens instinct, it obliterates the past. Totalitarianism is a cancer within the body of history, and (as such) obliterates distinctions.

Adapted from *'Totalitarianism'*, by Norman Mailer*

The trouble with *this* passage is not only is it densely written, as was Orwell's, but that most of it is *example or illustration*. These may be fascinating, but they are not 'key concepts', as anyone schooled in that old-fashioned exercise of précis will remember. Again, compare your list with mine:

> totalitarianism
> America

* Mailer, N. (1964) 'Totalitarianism', *The Presidential Papers*, Deutsch, London, pp. 181–186.

no-political-face
incubus
beheads
cancer
body-of-history
obliterates-distinctions

You will see that all my choices come from either the beginning or the end of the passage. There are two separate reasons for this.

(1) The brain/memory tends to work that way in a piece of *intensive* work of this kind – as we've observed. (See above, page 44.)
(2) The author's argument happens in this instance to be *designed* in such a fashion. The middle section develops, illustrates and explores an arresting opening statement, which is then summarized or confirmed in a number of dramatic definitions.

You may be surprised at the inclusion of '*incubus*' – and to be honest, I nearly missed it when preparing the exercise. But, if one thinks for a moment – and this exercise *depends* on one thinking while reading and noting – it is a vital word in the passage, from a number of angles. It evokes sorcery, something insidious, something invisible – all of them ideas that absolutely match the author's theory that totalitarianism has taken major root in America without many being aware of it. It also, of course, suggests something satanic and destructive, which thus establishes in addition the author's prime *value judgement*.

My other choices are, I think, more straightforward. Together, they offer a bald but comprehensible 'map' of the tone and topics of the argument. And again, each word or concept can be seen as a 'trigger' – a means of recalling and organizing the direction and over-all focus of the passage.

Paragraph 3
This is the hardest of the lot. The subject matter is difficult, and the writing – while admirably condensed and crisp – is sufficiently technical to seem opaque at first sight to even the most intelligent reader. Again, see how you fare reading it twice – though you may find you need to take it a little more slowly this time! The subject on this occasion is Economics – specifically, developments in trade between East and West.

In a time when the Eastern economic systems have retrograded into deepening crisis, barter-based cooperation, through licensing, buy-back, counter-purchase, co-production, joint association by partnership contract and joint ventures, is a life-saver. It may be the means of propping up the discredited elitists of the Eastern ruling class, composed of the Party, the bureaucracy and the KGB. To provide supportive Western technology without opening up Eastern systems to the variations of capital market forces certainly provides a breathing space, at least for the moment. Clearly the ruling caste itself has few anxieties about the possible consequences. They expect the capitalists to sell them the rope which may eventually hang them.

If cooperation, or economic detente, serves the aims of Eastern economic development without encroaching too harshly upon their flexible ideological barrage, the counter-ideologists of the West find the new arrangements equally easy to accommodate. For the monopoly capitalists or multinationals, detente has never been about avoiding nuclear war, nor about promoting constructive 'convergencies' between the best socialist and democratic features of both systems. Least of all has it been about injecting liberalism, human rights, and the market economy into the Communist countries. The motivation is entirely financial and secular: accumulating more profits and cash-flow by exploiting workers in the East in order better to exploit workers in the West. The business of big business is to make profits. The rulers of the East are making it their business to help them.

Adapted from *Vodka-Cola*, by Charles Levinson*

Tough, isn't it?! It may comfort you to know that, even after typing that passage slowly and carefully, I still find it very hard going. Nevertheless, I would say that the key words announce themselves clearly enough:

> cooperation
> life-saver
> Eastern ruling class
> few anxieties
> capitalists/sell/rope/hang
> *   *   *
> economic detente
> motivation
> financial

* Levinson, C. (1979) 'The Ideological Facade', *Vodka-Cola*, Gordon & Cremonesi, pp. 19–20.

> exploiting
> profits
> (Eastern) help

You'll note that I've cheated a little in the fifth and last choices. The former combines four separate words from one sentence, and the latter supplies an important clarifying adjective. Maybe you cheated a bit too – if so, good for you!

'Cheating' is in fact a silly word to use here. There are no *rules* about this method, and therefore cheating doesn't come into it. The idea is to note the controlling ideas and words so that they are as helpful as possible for *you*. You may even have spent longer than I suggested getting to grips with the passage: indeed, the exercise may this time have taken you a full (and arduous) fifteen minutes. That doesn't matter at all; and if you think fifteen minutes is a long time to spend on a relatively short (243 words) passage, then consider the following ego-boosting points:

(1) You've acquired at least a working knowledge of the main strands of a complex, difficult argument.
(2) You've progressed to this stage from absolute bewilderment in a very *short* time. From ignorance to familiarity in a quarter of an hour is good going!
(3) It is unlikely you'll ever have to read anything *more* difficult than this throughout your course; and the chances are that you will not encounter anything *as* difficult.

It's unlikely you'll ever have to read anything
more difficult

The truth is that if you stay alert, think while you read and note, and do not try to *master everything* right away, the technique of 'key word' noting rapidly promotes both knowledge and confidence.

This method also works well for note-taking in lectures, although you should not expect to isolate only the important key words in the lecture hall. There it is obviously better to write too many rather than too few. Whatever your strategy, you will have to look at the notes again in the evening to establish the *real* key words and concepts, and to even the notes out. Some points will need to be fleshed out, others condensed. Either way, much more of the lecture will 'come back to you' if you have a solid skeleton to build on, rather than something that may be all flesh and no bones.

Timing and duration

Key word noting is a highly intensive activity. You'll be only too well aware of that fact if you've just tried to do all three of the above paragraphs at one go. Indeed, one of the reasons why the last one was so tough was precisely because it was the *last*: you may have got the hang of the exercise by then, but it was probably cancelled out by the fatigue your brain was beginning to feel.

This is entirely normal, and as it should be. Early on in this book we noted that, regardless of intelligence-level or the activity undertaken, the brain performs best for about twenty to thirty-five minutes at a time. When the activity is as intensive as key word noting, it's to be expected that the brain will want to settle for the *lower* end of that span rather than the upper. So don't try to do too much in one session; and try to be in a relaxed and comfortable frame of mind when tackling the practice. Key word noting is a form of mental sprinting. The brain is asked to do a lot of work very fast; and, like a physical sprinter, it will perform best if it's nicely 'warmed up' and aware that it will be able to stop soon.

Codes and short-hand: inventing your own

I've already stressed that your private notes are for you alone. So it is both sensible and stimulating to adopt any method of abbreviation that suits you.

There are, of course, several established short-hand systems – Pitman's is probably the most famous. If you've been trained in one of these, that's fine. But if you haven't, you can construct your own with a little basic ingenuity. As with the advice I gave in the section on mnemonics, I believe it is better if I *don't* give you much illustration or offer you my own methods – not because I'm possessive about them, but because there's no reason to suppose that because they suit me they will suit *you*. However, by way of ignition:

(1) Use contractions and single-letter abbreviations wherever possible.

In an *essay* it looks both ugly and lazy to refer to, say, Shakespeare's *Henry Fourth Part Two* as *H4ii*; but in your private notes such a form is admirable, being both clear and quick.

(2) More ambitiously, try to work out a rapid number-reference system, where each digit represents a particular book/chapter/paragraph/whatever.

This is particularly useful, because in addition to highlighting specific areas of work, it organizes and clarifies your brain's 'filing system' generally.

(3) As with mnemonics, the more you can make a *game* out of time-saving and mind-clarifying methods, the better.

(4) I emphasized recently the potential value of 'doodling'. If you doodle naturally and unconsciously (and most of us do), you may find it worth while to *harness* such a practice to *conscious, concentrated work*. No matter if the alleged 'pattern' looks gibberish to everyone else: *you're* the only judge that matters. And if you can both have some fun doing this and record things of value, you'll find that the sense of doing 'conscious, concentrated work' fades rapidly, leaving you the most agreeable feeling of doodling for fun and profit.

Any method that gets you out of the rut of linear, carefully logical response should at least be tried; and I'll be surprised if you don't find it valuable. By broadening your approach, such methods broaden your thinking – with the frequent result that you hit upon ideas and a level of understanding that would have remained closed to you under a more 'formal' or allegedly 'correct' method.

Conclusion: note-taking at different stages

In a moment, we move on to essay planning and writing. Before we do, I want finally to emphasize that note-taking is, unlike essay-writing, a constant, *fluid* process. (I would use the term '*on-going*' if I didn't detest it so much.) Creative note-taking (i.e. for your own benefit) can and should happen at any and all stages of a piece of work. Let's list the most obvious:

(1) During initial reading (but probably best omitted during the intro-
     duction of a *lecture*).
(2) During confirmatory and developmental second reading, and
     during the rest of the lecture.
(3) Before writing the essay.
(4) *After* writing the essay/attending the lecture. A vital one, this, and
     one which even conscientious students too often omit.
(5) At any subsequent stage where review of existing notes prompts a
     new, further thought.
(6) During final revision, as both a clarifying aid and an ego-boosting
     demonstration that you *do*, after all, know/remember quite a lot!

None of these need take much time – especially (2), (5) and (6). They should, in fact, take precisely as much time, and be done in precisely the form, that you like. Clearly, when using the key word method, your job will be easier on (2) and (6) than on (1), since on those occasions the spotting of the key words will be confirmatory rather than identifying.

Good note-taking is a hugely valuable skill for any student. Good note-taking combines the recording of useful information with alert thinking. Provided these two criteria are met, it doesn't matter a jot how you do them, what they look like, or what use you put them to in the end. Some of your notes will become redundant before the end of your course: this is *not* proof of wasted time, but instead the clearest and happiest indication that you've grown beyond them – a process in which they played a vital, albeit temporary, part. For, to return to the two 'types' I sketched at the start, you should not 'grudge' the time spent taking notes, nor assume an attitude of 'reverence' about the activity. If you approach note-taking as a task solely for your benefit, you won't ever grudge the time, especially if you liberate yourself enough to employ methods which are lively and amusing. And if you remain alert and genuinely *thoughtful*, reverence won't be possible: you'll be discriminating and questioning as you note, and will thus move forward in your study far more commandingly. Notes *are* 'necessary', yes; but, thanks to methods and knowledge that Dr Johnson did not have available to him, there is no need to share his view of them as 'evils'. Nor, indeed, is there any excuse for doing so.

(*Nb* The section entitled *Energizing Patterns* in the next chapter (see pages 98–103) describes techniques that are also useful for note-taking.)

8

● ● ● ● ●

Crunch-time: essay planning and writing

When the day of judgement comes, we shall not be asked what we have read, but what we have done.

Thomas à Kempis

The above quotation is rather melodramatic, however seriously you take your study! Nevertheless, all proportion being kept, its doom-laden message corresponds to the feeling many students experience when they come to write an essay. It's a moment they dread: they are about to put their work and knowledge on the line, and such exposure cannot be put off any longer.

I am very sympathetic to this feeling – the more so since, to our shame, teachers rarely offer any systematic and fear-allaying advice on the matter. In trying to provide some such help, I'd like to stress one important point at once:

> **Just as there are different stages in and kinds of note-taking, there are various *types* of essay, each with their own purpose and value.**

In any course you will write a good many essays. (Scientists, it is true, do fewer than other disciplines; but even their essay-requirement is not negligible.) It should be self-evident that they will not all be of the same kind. It would be absurd to expect to produce the same kind of essay at the *beginning* of a course as those which you do at the *end* – including the exam. I'm not just talking about a difference in *quality*, but of *type*. Obviously, if your later essays *aren't* better, more assured, tighter and more knowledgeable than your efforts at the beginning, then something is wrong! No: I have in mind the need to tailor your essay to what you most need it to do *at that particular stage of your study* – a 'horses for courses' approach if you like.

Let's specify an example and look at it in detail. Imagine you've been set your first essay of the year. You've covered the work in class and in private; you've read a good deal of material; you've made various notes; and you've allowed time for the ideas to filter through and become tolerably familiar. Now you've got to write about it.

The essential first question to ask yourself is, 'Why?', or more precisely, 'What am I doing this essay *for*?'.

Now, a number of answers may occur to you, serious and facetious alike:

(1) Because the teacher needs some evidence that you *have* done the work.

(2) Because the teacher needs some evidence that *he's* done some work with, on, and for you, and that he's not being paid under false pretences.

(3) Because you need to find out just how much of the aforesaid work you really do know and *understand*.

(4) Because we are not brought into life for pleasure alone.

(5) Because until you commit yourself to some kind of 'test' on what you've done, it will be difficult to go on serenely to anything new.

(6) Because it's a uniquely profound and 'naked' way of digging into a subject: as someone once said, 'How can I know what I think until I've seen what I say?'.

Of these, (4) is a joke (that's the idea, anyway), and (2) is no more than half serious (although you'd be surprised how many teachers *do* feel under such pressure from time to time). (1) and (3) are I think reasonably obvious.

(5) and (6) are rarely thought of by anyone, especially (6). Yet it is perhaps the most important and valuable, above all at the *start* of a course. At that time, the essay is not so much a finished product as *part of the learning process*. Indeed, I would say that it is perhaps the *central* constituent of that process; and so, wherever possible, I would encourage students to look on those early written assignments as 'exploratory essays'. The virtues of such an approach are worth listing:

(1) If your main aim is to 'find out' through writing the essay, you will feel under far less pressure to arrange your material in an exact display – which is something you probably won't be able to do yet anyway.

(2) As a result, the *substance* of the essay will engage you much more than the *format*. This is exactly as it should be for most of the course. Eventually you will want and need to pay equal attention to both; but you can't achieve good style and structure until you're sure of what you want to say, and to establish *that* takes a good deal of time.

(3) It encourages you to take risks.

This is a creative and invariably profitable experience. Obviously, you have to be *sensible* about this: a wild-but-deliberate dive into a perverse or irrelevant argument is foolishly wasteful. But if you pursue your ideas in an honest and interested way, it won't matter that some of them don't convince, reach a dead end, or turn out to be 'red herrings'. At least you'll *know and understand* that they are not of value, and why they're not; and others *will* be highly productive, embodying insights and discoveries that the 'safer', restricted approach could never happen upon.

(4) Inevitably, you will include more material than is necessary. At this stage, that is an admirable fault, if indeed it is a fault at all. The further thinking and editing that flows from such work will help you to keep in close touch with your work, which as we've seen from Chapter 5 is an essential component of successful study.

(5) Some of such an essay's value will reside *in* its faults rather than *in spite of them.*

Ask yourself why every time you write
an essay

Speaking as a teacher, I find it far easier to help students by pointing out where they've gone wrong or somewhat awry than by trying to tell them what is *lacking* in the sense of *absent*. The former procedure has a mutually beneficial element of *dialogue* in it: it is the kind of thing that characterizes 'constructive criticism'. The latter, sadly, leaves no room for such dialogue. One can only point out what is missing – *without knowing whether the student understands why it's important or whether he will cover the necessary additions afterwards.*

The 'exploratory essay', therefore, allows you to *use* your teacher in a richer and more constructive way.

In case it strikes you as odd that I should look in detail at a special *kind* of essay before saying anything about basic planning and so on, I will end this section by underlining the primary point that

It is no use trying to plan an essay without first establishing what you're writing it for. The question 'why' should be the first word on any and every essay plan.

That's why I've looked at the 'exploratory essay' to start with. Its virtues (and its problems) demonstrate admirably where your priorities should lie, and how your planning-logic should operate.

Essay planning

How *not* to do it

Tell most students to construct an essay plan on a 'neutral' (i.e. applicable to all disciplines) topic such as 'Argue For Or Against Exams', and they would probably come up with something like this:

FOR   (1) Introduction.
            (2) Exams as a necessary test.
            (3) Exams as outside, 'objective' assessment. Standardization.
            (4) Exams as an opportunity to shine under pressure.
            (5) Conclusion.

Or – rather more likely in view of most students' opinions! – something like this:

AGAINST (1) Introduction.
            (2) Exams as unfair pressure.
            (3) Unjustified and distorting emphasis on speed.
            (4) Hostility of examiners.
            (5) Conclusion.

There are some useful ideas in both these plans, and I'm sure you could think of a number of others. (In case you can't, we go into the entire matter later in the book.) But neither plan is much use as a way of *igniting* or *fuelling* the essay itself. The middle sections are all right; but what about those bald words, 'Introduction' and 'Conclusion'? What help are they? Do they show you *how* to introduce and conclude your argument? Do they give you any idea of *what* they're going to say?

No, they don't, do they? And yet it is with the introduction that you hope to grab your reader's attention; and your conclusion will presumably be the final thrust that clinches his respect. There are no grounds for assuming that either will transpire out of such a plan. No thought's been given to how you will secure the reader's interest or finally persuade him; and that in turn will diminish the value of the sturdier middle sections.

I've seen a lot of essay plans like these; and most of them preface essays that, while often interesting and talented, have no real structure. They do not, in short, 'mirror' the alleged Plan at all. Such essays invariably begin with a couple of vacuous sentences that merely 'mark time' for the reader in a frustrating way. Sometimes it will be half a page or more before he reads the first point of any substance. All the previous material will have been for the *writer's* benefit – a way of 'winding himself up' into an argument just as one 'winds oneself up' into a long throw of a ball.

In such essays the conclusion is equally vapid. Rather than summing up the argument or, better still, producing its most telling point as an exhilarating exit, it merely repeats points already made, often in exactly the same words. Thus one starts with a yawn and ends with a sinking anti-climax.

Don't plan your essays like this. A good performance can only emerge from such a scheme if you're absolutely sure what you're going to say in every detail; and if you're *that* authoritative, you don't need a plan of any sort! Instead, bring your planning into line with the way essays *actually get conceived and written*, which I turn to now.

How and where to start

When you sit down to write an essay, you've usually got some idea about what you want to say and where you want to get to. You should be aware of such a general 'core' of material even if you're embarking on an 'exploratory essay'. (If you're not thus aware, it's very likely that you're not ready to start the essay yet.) In view of this, it makes perfect albeit paradoxical sense to say:

The best place to start an essay is *in the middle,* **or even, if you're sure enough of your material and argument,** *at the end.*

Of course, you won't present the essay in this form when you hand it in: that would be ludicrous. But an essay is a complex piece of work: while writing you have to focus on the title, marshal ideas, arrange them attractively, attempt to write crisp, pleasing English, and remain constantly alert to the threads of your argument, remembering what you've said and where you're heading. This adds up to a tough task, especially early in a course. So it is wise to begin where you are at your strongest – in the middle. When you've got some points down on paper, and the shape of your argument begins to unfold, *then* you can start thinking about your eventual introduction.

This method is what a 'rough draft' *ought* to be like – a kind of 'scissors-and-paste' job, comprising various sections and sentences which can be properly arranged once they are written down. You can inspect the material at leisure, 'shuffle' it, strengthen it, and begin to tie it together. At all costs you should try to avoid the commonest type of 'rough draft' that students do – that is, writing the essay in an 'orthodox' way in pencil or biro, and then copying out a 'neat', almost-word-for-word version to hand in. This is *virtually useless*, combining two dismal qualities that lack any fringe benefit: you learn nothing between drafts 1 and 2, and it takes a long joyless time.

Naturally, you haven't got time to use my suggested method *in an exam.* But the point is that if you've used your course-time properly, you won't have to anyway. Over the years you'll have learnt how to structure and write an essay under pressure. If you've experimented with techniques of the kind I'm suggesting, and used earlier essays sensibly as part of a review programme, you will by the exam be sufficiently the master of your material to adjust very fast to whatever question/title is thrown at you. For those who are less convinced about that, I deal with exam essay-writing in the later chapter on Examinations.

Essay writing

Introductions

I gave you one paradox just now: here's another.

The best time to write your introduction is right at the end.

'The man's a loony', I hear you muttering. But let me quote you an introduction I read in a recent Open University assignment. The question was 'Is religion indefinable?'. The student wrote:

> 'In order to answer this question adequately, it is first necessary to consider what religion is, and then to ascertain whether or not it can be clearly defined.'

I was sorely tempted to write a sarcastic 'good thinking!' in the margin. In the end, I simply drew the student's attention to the fact that *it says absolutely nothing*. All it does is offer an empty and unnecessary paraphrase of the question. Now, it's an excellent idea to *think* for a moment about what the question involves; but it is *not* a good idea to make such preliminary sorting-out the first thing your reader encounters.

Furthermore, it's most unwise to clutter up your style *at any time* with empty blocks of words such as 'it-is-first-necessary-to . . .' or 'in order to do *x*, we must first do *y*'. These may have a methodological strength in something like a Maths theorem; but in an essay they are simply boring. And it is particularly important not to allow your reader's first reaction to be a yawn or a groan. He may forgive (or even not notice) the odd clumsiness or empty phrase later; but at the beginning he will be at his most alert, his most hopeful and, conversely, his most severe.

If, however, you write your introduction *after* you've completed the main bulk of the essay, you'll be in a position to produce something vigorous and arresting. One of the finest essays I've ever marked was on Jane Austen's *Emma*, in response to the title, 'Examine Jane Austen's qualities as a social critic'. The material was excellent, with many crisp and invigorating insights. But what made it was the introduction. The student hit me right between the eyes with:

> 'Jane Austen knew a great deal about people, but nothing about sex. As a result, her social and moral vision is essentially *conservative*: ignorance of passion leads to a view of society that is founded on and celebrates order and good sense.'

The student was very bright, admittedly; but the real point about this introduction is not its textual intelligence so much as its *calculated* success at grabbing the attention. The student knew *exactly* what he was doing and the effect he wanted to achieve. He knew that, even if the reader turned purple with rage at such an opinion, he was nevertheless hooked; and he was sure enough about the soundness of his material to feel confident that he could demonstrate his argument clearly.

I asked him afterwards if he'd written the introduction last, as I suspected; and he had. He knew that the majority of his insights and judgements in the essay's core pointed to such a view, and so he chose to launch the essay with it. If you adopt the same method, you'll be surprised how immediately effective you can make your essays. At the very least, you won't ever waste your time and the reader's patience by taking half a page to make your first remark of any weight or purpose.

Conclusions

Similar considerations apply to conclusions as to introductions. What you want to avoid is anti-climax; so, for a start, cut out all such phrases as:

'In conclusion we can say that . . .'
'Thus it can be seen that . . .'
'By way of conclusion I would like to say that . . .'
'Thus, to conclude . . .'
'Thus, in answer to the question, we can safely say that . . .'

and so on. They say precisely nothing; they fall dully on the eye; and they are quite unnecessary anyway. In most cases, it's perfectly obvious that you've reached your conclusion – the writing stops a few lines down! So concentrate on saying something punchy instead.

How you achieve *that* is less straightforward, of course. You are, after all, summing up: it is not a good idea to introduce a completely new point at this stage (though, to be honest, such a policy is to be preferred to the kind of dull obviousness listed above). On the other hand, you want to avoid merely repeating things you've covered already, and you should *especially* avoid using the same words. Ideally, your conclusion should sum up your ideas and argument by 're-visiting' them in a fresh and economical way. Perhaps I might quote again from that *Emma* essay to show you what I mean:

'Jane Austen seems to have been serenely confident about the values in which she had been brought up. Unlike her near-contemporary, Emily Brontë, there is in Austen no sense of inner conflict about what is right and true: the strength of her books and their moral outlook lies in her certainty. This confidence is never righteous, because of her compassion and humour; but it does mean that her social criticism, for all its authority, is based on a belief that, at root, her society was a just and good one. Radical alternatives never occurred to her, because they lay outside her experience and imagination.'

Let's list the virtues of that conclusion:

(1) It is contentious (as was his introduction): it could cause violent disagreement. But that is its strength: it engages the reader's full attention, and assumes a kind of dialogue with him.

(2) It is logical and true-to-itself. In no sense does it repeat the introduction, but it does *match* it impressively.

(3) The use of a comparison (Emily Brontë) is invigorating, inviting the reader to consider the book in a broader context, and thus extending the debate beyond the essay.

(4) It is tautly written and freshly phrased.

(5) It is *short*: long rambling conclusions are always a mistake, no matter how much interesting material they contain.

(6) It is, according to your point of view, stimulating or challenging: it asks the reader to think a little.

You might be fearful of producing such a conclusion, in case it was read by a rabid Austenphile who'd regard any implicit criticism of his heroine as a major heresy. All I can say is that, however much a reader might disagree with or even dislike such an argument, it would be a harsh and stupid one who would 'mark it down' as a result. Just remember this: few if any students are ever penalized for being interesting. So try to make your conclusions muscular and compelling, using the principles I've listed above. *Anything* is better than a tired rehearsal of points and phrases the reader has already digested.

Advanced essay-writing

An unwise model

When I first went into the sixth form, one of my teachers gave us this elementary model for planning our essays:

(a) Say what you're going to say.

(b) Say it.

(c) Say you've said it.

This was good advice *at the time*. We were beginners; we were struggling with lots of new material; such a bald, basic pattern helped us to achieve some kind of structure in our arguments.

The model soon becomes redundant, however. Worse, it can easily promote the kind of flaws I've already discussed – obvious and dull writing, stagnation, anti-climax, and a general impression of plodding. Its emphasis on clear logic is a good thing to *bear in mind*, as it keeps you focussed on how your essay is unfolding. But it does not have to be spelt out *in the writing*.

Once you've acquired a degree of familiarity with the material, and with it an increased confidence and fluency, your methods should go beyond such 'cat-sat-on-the-mat' procedures. 'Exploratory essays' can profit from such a pattern, certainly: these are written, after all, when you're still getting to grips with the material. But now you've reached the later stage where your essays are a *performance* rather than *a form of enquiry*, you must have your 'audience' constantly in mind. 'Advanced' essay-writing is synonymous with 'performing': your purpose is not only to prove your competence but also to *entertain* – to interest, stimulate and even enchant. If you take your reader on a dreary guided tour of basic logic, he won't be too enthralled. Neither, come to that, will you.

Linking, digging and polishing

I've just advised you to beware of boring the reader by taking him through over-obvious, unnecessary steps in the basic logic of your essay's *structure*. But you must also, as a writer of sophisticated essays, be careful not to *omit* steps in the logic of your *argument*. It is one thing to assume that he knows without needing to be told that you're starting the essay, moving on to another point, finishing: such omissions are sensible and indeed essential if you don't want to irritate him. But it's quite a different matter if you leave out an important link between two points, leaving *him* to do the work. *That* is equally annoying. So, while sparing the reader a dull, unfruitful survey of your essay's architecture, don't overdo it by insisting that he supply the bridges between your *ideas*. Always make sure that your argument progresses clearly and comfortably for the reader. It is not quite enough to put down two related points without *showing* that they are linked, and why. Very often, you will need nothing more than a simple conjunction (which means 'linking with'), such as 'so', 'thus', or even 'and'.

Essays whose material is not properly linked acquire a bland, almost unfinished, quality: the same is true of essays where the writer doesn't 'dig' into his material with quite enough depth or penetration. As a result, the points lie on the surface, as if waiting for the reader to mine them properly. Don't let *this* happen in your essays, either. Explore and develop your points as far as you can – don't, as so many students do, settle for the first and second useful ideas that occur to you. If you're talented enough to think of those (and nearly all students are) then a little vigorous turning over the ground is very likely to lead to a third,

Read your essays critically and remove 'flab' and
emptiness

and a fourth. Time and again I read quite good essays which, with a little more penetration or enquiry, could have been *very* good. 'Linking' and 'digging' are closely related, in that the writer who concentrates fiercely on ensuring that his points flow lucidly from one to the other will very probably find that such a clarity of focus sponsors further, more telling, ideas.

Finally, you should always read your essays over *critically* – that is, in the position of the *reader* rather than you the *writer*. Look them over closely: have you *really* said what you *thought* you'd said? Any uncertainty in your answer, and you should clarify the material. For something to be 'more or less there' or implicit in your writing won't do: it's got to be unambiguously out in the open. Look, too, for any 'flab' and emptiness, thus ensuring that the style is as taut as you can currently make it. To 'polish' essays in this way is a pleasant experience, and one which can make a lot of difference to their final impact and quality. Furthermore, to get into the habit of 'polishing' will prove highly profitable in an exam.

(Appendix A offers some specific pointers on style and use of English, and Christopher Turk's chapter on computers also has some extremely good advice on the psychology and practice of writing.)

Energizing patterns: reducing the thought-gap

This section could well have appeared earlier in the chapter, because 'energizing patterns' are useful at the very start of essay-planning and writing. I've delayed it because, in addition to offering you a new technique, it serves as a kind of summary to all that I've said about note-taking and even reading, as well as specific essay matters.

One problem that all students have is that their thoughts are so much faster than their writing-speed. This is a fact of being human, and in crude approximate figures the disparity can be expressed thus:

(a) Some thought is electronic, and can reach speeds of 100 miles per *second*.

(b) Most thought is chemical, and therefore slower: even so, the speed involved is around 190 miles per hour (*c.* 300 km.p.h.).

(c) Even a fast writer will not cover the page at more than five miles per hour.

I call this 'The Thought Gap'. We've all had the experience of thoughts escaping us before we've had time to 'pin them down' in writing; and very frustrating it is too. But sometimes we fail to register them because we try to write down too much – a whole sentence or logical phrase rather than just a word or even a sign. 'Energizing patterns', as I call them, by-pass such laborious and wasteful procedures, and narrow the chasm between the respective speeds of thinking and writing.

A thought-gap: thinking is faster than writing

As an initial demonstration, since this chapter is about essay-writing, let us suppose you have been set an essay on 'The Cruel Sea'. It's probably quite a while since you did a 'composition' of this sort, but no doubt you remember the task well! The 'normal' practice is to think about it for a while until a good idea arrives; to 'chew over' that idea and reflect on ways in which it could be developed; and then to sit down and start the story/essay.

This can of course be quite successful; but it has one huge built-in disadvantage. If you simply wait for an idea to arrive, the over-whelming likelihood is that you'll use the *first* good idea that occurs to you; and although the first *may* be the best, it's more than possible that the second or third ideas would have been better. Best of all, you might havè been able to *combine all three* in a thoroughly rich and satisfying way.

As an alternative to that 'normal' method, why not try *trapping* your thoughts on paper from the very beginning? This may – indeed, almost certainly will – stimulate *further* thoughts very fast.

$$\boxed{\text{THE CRUEL SEA}}$$

Fig. 8.1   (a) Energizing patterns: the start.

You can do it like this. Take a piece of paper, and write 'The Cruel Sea' in the middle. Put a 'box' round it. Your piece of paper now looks like Fig. 8.1(a). 'Big deal', you might feel like saying. But just focus on that central box, and let your mind mull it over. As soon as any idea comes, write it down – use a 'railway line' approach, sending different 'themes' or 'angles' in different directions so as to keep them distinct. Then, if and when you've got about four or five 'main lines', look at each one in turn and see how many 'branch lines' or sub-themes you can get from each one. *Use single words or even abbreviations wherever possible.* The emphasis is solely on speed, on pinning down a thought before it vanishes.

Using this method, you'll be amazed how fast you cover your piece of paper. Look at Fig. 8.1(b), where you'll find my own effort, which took me five minutes.

PLEASE STUDY FIG. 8.1(b) FOR A FEW MOMENTS

Because this is a book, the pattern is quite neat: I can assure you that the original was much more of a mess! Tidiness is wholly irrelevant and unnecessary. The only thing that matters is that you should be able to

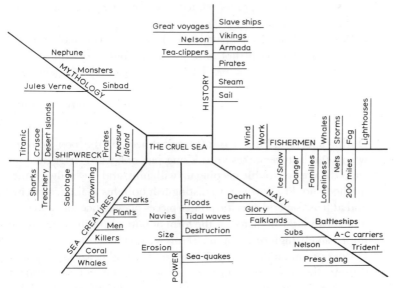

Fig. 8.1   (b) Energizing patterns: ten minutes later.

decipher your pattern when you come to consider it more sedately. While *doing it*, you should simply try to get down as much as crosses your mind as fast as you can.

The marvellous thing about this technique is that after just five or ten minutes, you have a host of ideas that you can now brood on as slowly as you like, and you have a large, rich *choice*. No longer is there any danger that you'll settle for the first decent idea that occurs to you: having worked so fast and productively, you can now afford to decide which 'angle' you most like. Moreover, you're in a position to *see connections between the themes*. In Fig. 8.1(b), for example, there are links between the various 'branch lines'/sub-themes in 'SHIPWRECK' and 'HISTORY', 'SEA CREATURES' and 'FISHERMEN', and so on. The links are elementary, agreed; but they *visually* suggest ways in which you can combine and enrich your material, be it for an essay or a story.

'Energizing patterns' are equally valuable in advanced essays. Again, you put your chief concept (perhaps the essay's title, reduced if possible to one word) in the central box, let your mind wash over it, and record as many of the resulting ideas as you can. When you peruse the pattern afterwards, you'll not only have a lot of potential material, but a clear visual signal of the connections you can make. With such a visible reminder, your subsequent essay should be more fluent as well as more substantial, its points related to each other in a comfortable and persuasive fashion.

The greatest value of such patterns is that they start you off, quickly and enjoyably. They will not *solve* problems; but they will at least identify what the problems *are*. They have other major benefits too. Because the method is so simple, it is also very versatile – a pattern can be used for whatever you like, whenever you like. Here are some possible uses:

(1) During a lecture. Put the title/central concept in the 'box', and see where the lecturer takes you. Using just one-word 'triggers' you should have no trouble keeping up with him, and the 'railway line' method should allow you to distinguish both his main arguments and at least several specific points/pieces of evidence for each one. These can later be listed in the form of notes, and thus ensure an impressively high recall of the lecture's substance.

(2) During private note-taking. I don't myself find it works very well during the *first* reading/note-taking; but on all subsequent occasions it is most useful. If you look again briefly at Fig. 8.1(b), you will see that it looks very much like a 'creative doodle' such as I advocated in the last chapter.

(3) When key word noting. You can adapt that method to include lines or *any* kind of visual linking, which will endorse and clarify the key words' importance.

(4) At the start of a revision session. Do a quick 'energizing pattern' on as much of the material as you can recall, and you will shortly have a definite picture of what you know, and therefore of what you need to refresh your memory about.

(5) As a skeletal plan for an exam answer. You haven't got time to do the kind of detailed planning I describe in the previous section; but you *can* afford the few minutes needed to do a pattern of this kind. This will get you confidently started, and also serve as an invaluable reminder of what you want to say – something easily forgotten when under exam pressure.

If you are anxious to know more about these 'patterns', Tony Buzan's book *Use Your Head** has a lot of interesting and lively material on them. He calls them 'creative patterns': I've 'rechristened' them, because strictly speaking they are not creative at all. They *sponsor* creativity by giving you a rapid and exciting ignition – hence my use of 'energizing'. The best term for them, perhaps, might be 'useful mess'!

* Buzan, *op. cit.*

Out of their apparent chaos, your mind makes order and purpose. Such a transition cannot but boost your confidence, and thus makes the subsequent tasks more fun and more successful.

Conclusion: a check-list of guidelines

Essays are the centre of your work: that's why students are often so nervous about them. As a summary, I've listed some of the things you'd do well to remember or consider. If you enjoy your course, then you ought to enjoy writing on or for it most of all: I hope these suggestions help you to do so.

(1) Always try to be clear as to *why* you're doing the essay.

(2) Try to think of the essay as a central part of your learning rather than *solely* as a finished product/public document. This is especially advisable during the first half of your course.

(3) Until you're master of your material (i.e. in the last quarter of your course at the earliest), start your preparation in the middle.

(4) Practise writing your introduction after you've completed everything else.

(5) Ensure your conclusion is not damply repetitive of earlier ideas and phrases.

(6) *Think* all the time, and particularly about the words you use. Ask yourself if the phrase you're contemplating is really as good as you can make it, or indeed whether you need it at all. Avoid clichés, and above all avoid time-marking sentences that say nothing.

(7) Make sure that related points really *are* linked, and not merely implicit. You can't afford to hope that the reader will *infer* an idea or a connection: you must ensure that it's there for him to see.

(8) Always pause before embarking on a fresh argument or theme, checking that you've got all you can out of the previous one. Very often, a few moments' reflection will lead you on to further points that lift the material from the merely satisfactory to the truly authoritative.

(9) Plan your essay in any way that is valuable to you. It's probably best to do it informally; but whatever you do, jettison any notion that the plan is part of the essay as a public document. Your plan is totally private, and is useful only in so far as it helps you focus, organize, and tighten your material.

(10) *Read* as many essays as you can stand – especially those of your fellow students. You will ultimately learn more from each other than from anyone else.

If you follow all, or even most, of these, within six months you should be writing good essays. Furthermore, you'll be doing so almost instinctively, as a habit. Once you've regularly switched on to what you're doing and why, you will *think* much more efficiently, and that will improve everything about your writing.

9
● ● ● ● ●

Teachers and how to use them: a student's view

Chris Pope

How often have you sat in a classroom, bored to tears, thinking how much more progress you would be making if you were alone? Often, I should imagine! Certainly, some lessons are a complete waste of time, and with the range of textbooks available it is possible to study virtually anything on your own.

But have you ever tried mastering a subject without any kind of help *at all*? Possible though it may be, to do so is to choose the harder option – and the chances are very much that when you finish, your knowledge of the subject will be worse than if you had had a tutor. Worse, that is, both in quantity and quality of knowledge. If you don't believe me, try it out! And if you genuinely do better on your own than with a teacher, it's either because you're exceptional or, more likely, because you are not using your teacher properly. Even a lousy teacher is better than nobody! These next few pages will, I hope, assist you in making full use of your teachers, and thus persuade you that they are a great help.

There are two main reasons why teachers are better than textbooks. One is that they are flexible, and can adapt to your particular needs and problems, which a book obviously can't do. And, probably more important, the second is that communication between two human beings is far better than that between a book and a human being. Having said that, it is usually the latter that causes all the problems! And it's not just we students who are to blame – some teachers' methods leave a lot to be desired. I'm sure you will have, at some time or other, come across teachers that approximate to the following two stereotypes.

The Spoon-Feeder

For the Spoon-Feeder, any topic not on the exam syllabus is a waste of time. His lessons are an exercise in reducing the amount of thinking, both for the teacher and the student, to the minimum necessary to pass the exam. The Spoon-Feeder will therefore use the same notes year in, year out, and dictate them word for word. Homework is set at the end of each lesson, to be collected in at the beginning of the next; and every so often there will be some form of test to ensure that material is actually being absorbed. For the student, all that needs to be done is to assume a fixed look of fascination and let the pen do the rest!

Spoon-Feeders come in all shapes and sizes. Some are extremely able, or were so at one time; some are hardly more proficient than the students they teach – hence their almost manic reliance on their notes and on an absolute, fixed programme in their lessons. Most of them are solidly competent, and they will get you through all right. But if you want to succeed fully (as opposed to 'get by'), you'll need to find a way of getting more vigorous help than such a style offers. For a Spoon-Feeder is primarily concerned with supplying you with the answers: he's not terribly interested in the questions themselves, or in enquiry as an activity. A truly Advanced Spoon-Feeder is a breathing, fleshed-out version of Coles' Notes – no more, no less.

Stereotype : a teacher who spoon-feeds

The Prolix Professor

The Prolix Professor is always in a muddle, and tends to live in a world of his own. He is highly intelligent, and has an interest in everything . . . except the syllabus in hand. Never having had any difficulties with the subject himself, he finds it hard to see where other people's problems lie and thus how to help them. His obsession with obscure topics and his unparalleled ability to digress results in the structure of his lessons being rather like that of scrambled egg. It is frequently impossible to follow him, and any notes taken during the lesson stand a high chance of being incomprehensible. Worse still, should a question be asked, the answer is more likely to confuse than help.

The Prolix Professor is invariably enthusiastic, and usually kindly, and so he is liked, rather as one always feels a certain fondness for 'a character'. But he poses equal, if opposite, problems to the student relieved to escape the Spoon-Feeder. Instead of a narrow, drily competent Gradgrind, you now labour under a chaotic Brainstawm. Spoon-Feeder gave you dull, concentrated exam-fodder; Prolix Professor offers you a cascade of bewildering bubbles with no core and no substance. Any student unlucky enough to draw two such figures simultaneously finds that his study approximates a diet made up solely of salt beef and ship's biscuits on the one hand, and candy floss soufflés on the other!

Of course, most teachers fall somewhere between these two extremes, and in any case a teacher will use different styles and tactics depending on the class, the subject he has to teach, and the time available to him. However, 'seeing through' the method used should help communication, and also increase your sense of security and thus confidence.

It will also determine your note-taking strategy. Since Chapter 7 has already dealt with note-taking in detail, all I need stress is its importance during lessons. No matter how interested you are and how well a lesson may be going, you will probably forget a good deal, if not most, of the material by the following morning, let alone the end of the year! Your notes, unlike someone else's notes or a textbook, will be an invaluable reminder. (If the lesson is incomprehensible and/or excruciatingly tedious, note-taking will keep you awake!) It is then up to you to make sense of these notes in the evening, and to rewrite them if necessary.

It is *crucial* to understand everything that you study; and it's important for you to be honest with yourself about the term 'understand'. It doesn't mean the vague grasping of a situation, but being fully comfortable and clear about it. Only you know if you have truly understood something, when a problem suddenly resolves itself and the penny drops. Being able to regurgitate facts is pointless unless you can make use of them; and before you can do that you must have first understood the situation/context. Indeed, your success at a course depends on how well the inevitable gap that exists between two human beings has been bridged. This is achieved by facts and issues being well presented by the teacher and your understanding the problems involved.

I realize that this is easier said than done. Understanding sometimes requires a great deal of thought: it can also take a fair time – longer, perhaps, than you have in the lesson. But if you solve a problem yourself (with help) instead of merely being told how to do it, not only are you much more likely to remember it next time, but you will then be considerably better prepared for the next step. A Chinese proverb sums it up concisely and well:

'Hear and forget; see and remember; do and understand.'

It is always preferable to try to sort out any difficulties on your own, even if it does take a long time. Often, if the solution doesn't come after a while, it is worth taking a break and returning to it later. It's extraordinary how something will suddenly become clear the following morning!

Nevertheless, there are times when you find yourself well and truly stuck/fogged/stagnant, the prisoner of a problem that will *not* sort itself out. It is at this point that the way in which you use your teacher is important. With a good teacher, such times should be less frequent than with a bad one; so the worse the teacher, the more the responsibility for your success lies with you! Whatever your luck in this respect, one thing is paramount, and a constant whatever the quality of teaching you receive: if there is something you don't understand, you *must* ask, again and again if necessary, until you do understand it – *fully*. Obvious though this may seem, it is almost incredible how many people would rather sit in silent ignorance than admit to not understanding. What is the point of embarking on a topic if you're not going to understand it? And what is the point of mutely implying understanding when you have no real idea of what is being talked about? To behave in such a way is the only *truly stupid* thing a student can do: it's a form of false pride, which is about the most useless, damaging quality anyone can have, let alone a student!

You should try, if possible, to locate *exactly* where your problem lies and ask a clear, concise question that begs a direct answer. This helps everyone: the class (as it saves time); the teacher (as he knows precisely where you require help); and above all you (as you are more likely to get the answer you need). If you really can't understand the explanations, or the teacher turns out to be incompetent, then you will need to ask someone from the class who *has* understood, or, if necessary, another teacher. With perseverance, you will get there eventually!

And remember, as Richard Palmer stresses in the next chapter: teachers are *paid* to be asked questions and to answer them. It is one of the main parts of their job; and any teacher who discourages questions is not merely lousy – he is, to a certain extent, failing to fulfil his professional duty. Fortunately, such figures are rare: most teachers *like* being asked questions, and are only too anxious to help you. Sometimes, even the best teachers won't be able to give you an immediate, clear answer: after all, nobody knows everything! But if you regard your teacher as a guide and even a friend, you will 'use' him far more successfully and sensibly than by sitting in passive silence wondering what on earth he's going on about.

10

• • • • •

Teachers and how to use them: a teacher's view

He who can, does; he who cannot, teaches.
G. B. Shaw

This chapter is really a postscript to the previous one, for Chris has said most of what I would want to say on the subject. All I want to do in these few pages is offer some endorsing amplification of the points he made, from the 'other side' of the classroom.

I freely admit to being at times either a Spoon-Feeder or a Prolix Professor, and I'm sure that most teachers would recognize at least a few of their past lessons in Chris's caricatures! (Indeed, I once taught a lesson so ineffably dull that *I* fell asleep in it, in mid-sentence.) But, as he says, teachers who *regularly* match either of his portraits are, fortunately, rare. There are a few teachers around bored by all students, and there are also a few others who have no interest or even competence in their subject. But there aren't many of either.* Most teachers are skilled professionals who enjoy what they do and consider it important, and thus thoroughly and rightly resent the fatuous remark quoted above.

I'm not being quite as pompous and flag-waving as that last sentence might suggest. For implicit in Shaw's epigram† are two very damaging notions – damaging, that is, to any *student* who chooses to regard the

---

* Having said that, if you *are* unlucky enough to get a teacher who is interested neither in you nor in his subject, there is only one sensible thing to be done – transfer to another class. I am well aware that this is easier said than done; but it's the only way, finally. If you're getting absolutely nowhere under his guidance (or lack of it), it makes no sense to remain miserable and uninstructed; and perhaps it's only right that others should know.

† To be fair to Shaw, the remark is given to his hero in *Man and Superman*, John Tanner, a man more distinguished for *bon mots* than for any real sense or achievement.

remark as anything more than a faded shallow witticism. The first is the implication that *anyone* can teach, just like that; and the second is the suggestion that there is something intrinsically inadequate and sterile about teaching as an activity. Any student who even vaguely subscribes to either sentiment stands little or no chance of getting the best use out of his teachers – and thus considerably limits his chances of success and enjoyment from the start.

Contrary to certain beliefs, *not* everyone can teach. For a start, you have to *like* children and/or their elder counterparts, students. No doubt there are a few misanthropes infesting the odd staffroom here and there – people who dislike schools, children and all term-hours between nine and four: they deserve to be pitied as well as despised, because they must have a rotten life. In addition, you have to like your subject, and to know it properly: it is only a matter of time before any intelligent student will ask a question that requires more knowledge than what can be nervily mugged-up the night before the lesson.

I stress all this for one reason only: it is essential that you regard your teachers as helpmeets, guides and, as Chris suggested, *friends*. They are not gods; they are not infallible. Neither do they regard you as idiots, pests, or absolute disciples. Like everyone with a set of skills, they enjoy using them well; and using their skills well means helping you to learn and grow. Very few good teachers are remotely envious: it is *exciting* to encounter a mind better than one's own and to help it develop. And once you realize that teachers are on your side, professionally committed to helping you, and respectful of you as an individual, you will already be well on the way to achieving the kind of profitable communication that Chris wisely defines as the major benefit of being taught.

So, as he says, *never be afraid to ask*. Teachers are paid to answer questions: it is, in a way, the biggest part of their job, and only an idiot or a Basil Fawlty-type neurotic ever resents those who ask him to do what he's paid for. There is only one thing that *really* annoys a teacher, and that is outlined in the 'playlet' below.

Teacher:	Right. Does everyone understand that?
Class:	*Tacit*
Teacher:	Anyone at all unsure? I don't *mind* if you are – I just need to know.
Class:	*Tacit*
Teacher:	Sure? *(Pause)* Okay, on to the next topic . . .

ONE WEEK LATER

Teacher: Okay, we covered this last week satisfactorily, and you all understood it, so you shouldn't have any trouble with it. *(Pause as he sees blank/worried/ bewildered/panic-struck faces.)* What's the matter?

Brave Student: I don't understand this at all.

Other Students: Nor me/Or me/Me neither/What's it all about?/ Etc.

Teacher: AAAAAARRRRRRGGGGGGHHHHHH!!!!!

You can't blame him for screaming, can you? It's partly frustration: a whole week's work has just been shown to be largely wasted, since it's hardly likely that they've understood succeeding lessons if they failed to grasp the original material. But it's mainly a bellow of rage at the sheer stupidity of remaining in silent ignorance when given a friendly opportunity to voice any doubts, problems, or gaps in understanding.

Chris terms such behaviour false pride, and I agree with him. I am, I hope, always sympathetic to the shy student, and I do understand how difficult it seems sometimes to admit ignorance and thus risk being 'shown up' in front of others. But if you truly want to learn, such a wallflower approach is a luxury you cannot afford. Indeed, to stay silent when perplexed is positively crippling.

So ask your questions – as many and as often as you like. If they are serious and honest enquiries, no teacher will ever get impatient with you. For remember this:

No teacher can help you efficiently unless he is first aware of what you *don't* know and *don't* understand.

It's easy to preach to the converted, and even easier to teach the already knowledgeable. There isn't, however, much *point* to it: the teacher's chief function, and his main pleasure, is to help you to master what you didn't know before.

There is one further point about student questions that Chris didn't cover – not surprisingly, because it is entirely to do with teacher reaction. It is this: teachers are themselves learning as they teach, and questions and ideas from their students can – indeed, often do – throw a new light on their subject. Good questions are a delight to any committed teacher: they stretch him, and frequently expand his own knowledge and awareness as a result. So, far from worrying whether you're being a pest when you raise a query or an idea, remind yourself instead that you are *adding* to your teacher's enjoyment of the lesson and his over-all insight.

You may think that sounds rather too idyllic; but I can assure you that it's a lot more realistic than the desire 'not to be a nuisance'. A personal anecdote may help convince you. I have now been teaching the same Open University course for seven years. (The Foundation Arts Course, involving six disciplines.) It's a good course; but several students have asked me how I can stand doing the same material year in, year out. The answer is that it is *never* the same material from one year to the next – *because of the students*. Their reactions are always different, and so are their problems. Most of all, their questions are individual and therefore invariably *new*; and so the basic material from which I work and which I cover is made fresh every year. In short, the material *would* have become unacceptably tedious a long time ago were it not for you lot out there! Chris stressed the importance of friendly communication between student and teacher: I can go a little further, and say that you will greatly *help* your teacher if you make the best use of him – in all sorts of ways.

It is now appropriate to consider some of the things teachers *can't* do for you and which you should not expect.

For a start, no *one* teacher can do it all, however superb. Within our subjects we all have *particular* enthusiasms, areas of expertise, favourite areas; and, consequently, we all have certain blind spots, areas we know less well, and even prejudices. This is inevitable and normal, and you shouldn't worry about it. You should, however, canvass other views and ideas whenever you can. Your teachers will encourage this anyway; and they *mean* it – it's not just idle professional courtesy. These days, more and more courses use team-teaching, or at least an element of pluralism: this is a sensible and valuable development, and you should extend it wherever possible. It is pleasing to be asked things by students other than one's own: most teachers are to some extent born show-offs, and they're always happy to increase their audience!

Chris also encouraged you to ask fellow students, and I couldn't agree with him more. Indeed, in the end you will learn more from each other than from us, your teachers: you all *live* the same problems and the same learning experience, and therefore share a language that is more immediate and more profound than that which you share with even the friendliest teacher. Read each other's essays; compare notes; work on problems together. You will find it fun, and thereby extremely productive.

There is one thing no teacher can do for you, nor is there any reason why he should even try: to make you work. When you're younger, and still legally required to attend lessons, it is perhaps not unreasonable to expect your teacher to nag you about undone homework and so on. But once you *choose* to do a course (and this book is written for voluntary students), it is no part of your teacher's job to chase you for work that you're doing *for yourself*. If you can't be bothered to do a piece of work and you are not nagged about it, don't ask yourself what the teacher thinks he's doing, letting you get away with it. Instead, ask yourself what *you* think you're doing, not completing work you've made a free decision to undertake. Up to the age of 16, students can expect to be 'policed' in this way: it's part of the teacher's responsibility to ensure that you cover the work you're compulsorily in school to do. After that, if *you* can't be bothered, it's absurd to expect him to be.

Finally, however closely you work with your teachers, it is important to stay independent. Up to a point, of course, you are dependent on their skill, their knowledge, and their breadth of understanding. Beyond that point, however, you must be careful to stay yourself. It is almost certain that somewhere along the line you will not see absolutely eye to eye with your teacher about an idea, an interpretation, a method. This is, admittedly, disconcerting when it happens; but it is a good thing. It clearly shows you that you're developing, and have a mind of your own. So keep hold of that awareness. Indeed, such a quality is one of the fundamental characteristics of the truly academic mind, and leads me to a most important distinction.

'Academic *versus* 'studious'

It is widely assumed that these two words are synonymous: in fact, in a subtle way, they are virtual opposites. 'Academic' is a vigorous concept; while 'studious' is, finally, a negative or, rather, passive one. 'Academic' connotes someone who can *think*, make his own judgements and connections, and for whom study is an exciting exploration – of the self as well as the material. On the other hand, 'studious' – while admirable, and a necessary *prerequisite* of all good academic work – describes a conscientious but sponge-like mind that absorbs but does not give out anything of note. To a teacher, there is nothing more exciting than a genuinely academic mind, and nothing duller than a *merely* studious one.

All academics are bound to disagree sooner or later – and that includes students. Staying independent in such a fashion does not involve or require arrogance: it is of course idiotic to dismiss someone simply because you disagree with them on one or two matters. (If we all did that, we'd have no friends, nor even acquaintances.) But just as I'm sure *you* won't do such a thing, remember that your teacher won't either. Hardly any teachers are Jean Brodie types: they are not interested in moulding students to an exact specification, and still less do they want their classes to comprise junior clones of themselves. They simply want to help you learn; and that includes learning what *you* like, feel, and consider valuable.

11

• • • • •

Sources and resources

The mark of an educated man is that he's prepared to look things up.
Kingsley Amis

Chris Pope and I have both made the point that no teacher, no matter how clever and how kind, can be expected to know *everything*. Sooner or later, you are going to have to go elsewhere for some of your information, and also for additional stimulation.

I am aware that telling someone to 'look it up' is much easier said than done. Very often, I'm afraid, it is the remark of a tired, irritated or just ignorant teacher; and it is often more or less useless as advice. For the point is, obviously, that no-one can 'look something up' unless they first know *how* and *where* to do so. I hope this chapter, elementary though it is, will leave you better equipped for independent enquiry.

I shall be looking at the following resources and techniques:

(1) Reference books.
(2) Libraries.
(3) Periodicals.
(4) The interpretation of reading-lists.
(5) Bookshops.
(6) Abstracts and indexes.
(7) Personal indexes.

Reference books

These are best divided into dictionaries and thesauruses on the one hand, and the remainder on the other.

Dictionaries and thesauruses
There is a profusion of such publications available nowadays, and the majority of them are first-class. But in order to get proper use out of a

good dictionary, you've got to know *how* to use it; and this, as with so much else in study, means *thinking sensibly.*

Let's take an example. Suppose you need to find out exactly what the phrase 'professional foul' means. Even a good dictionary (e.g. the Concise Oxford) will not necessarily spell it out for you; so you've got to think a bit. It isn't good enough to imagine that the two commonest meanings of the adjective, 'engaged in for money' or 'proper to one's profession', can be simply applied in this case: to associate 'foul' with the first makes little sense, and to pair it with the second seems outrageously contradictory. The use cannot be fully grasped until the underlying *concept* has been at least partially understood – that the foul is committed because there is money or some kind of professional pride at stake. In other words, *both* those two meanings are involved – dubiously entangled to make an act of cynicism seem somehow more forgivable.

Another example can usefully be taken from a foreign language. It is remarkable how many quite good linguists commit absurdities to paper, *because they haven't worked out what the* English *means first.* Take the sentence:

He has ideas above his station.

The incautious linguist may well translate this as:

Il a des idées au-dessus de sa gare.

This well-known howler is ludicrous, of course. But note that it is *not* because the translator is poor at French (not necessarily, anyway): it's because he didn't think enough about the *English* metaphor he was dealing with. As a result, he confuses the distinct meanings of 'railway/ bus halt' and 'social position', with inevitably humiliating consequences.

So the best advice I can give you in the preliminary use of dictionaries is this:

Use them with *intelligence.* **They are not oracles or magic founts of wisdom: they are** *tools* **which must always be applied with care and thought.**

Naturally, there will be times when your own intelligence, however well applied, is not enough. *That* is the time to ask – a teacher, a friend, anyone who might know the answer. But if you do keep your mind in charge, and not merely expect the dictionary to yield up its secrets like some verbal Slave of the Ring, you'll find the times when you need to ask getting fewer and fewer.

Much the same principle governs use of thesauruses – except that there you must be even more careful. A thesaurus, by definition, lists groups of words that have a broadly similar meaning. But it is only a valuable aid if you think very alertly about the possible *differences* between the words as well as their similarities. Consider, for example, these synonyms for the word 'break':

> shatter
> demolish
> interrupt
> crack
> fracture

Yes, they all mean 'break'; but look at how idiotic these sentences are:

> To make an omelette, first demolish four eggs. . . .
> He interrupted his leg while ski-ing.
> The pile-driver fractured the shop-window.
> We shattered our journey at a motorway café.

More seriously, there is for example a great difference between 'fracturing' a bone and 'shattering' it, or between 'cracking' one's knuckles and 'demolishing' them. Unless you work out beforehand some idea of the *strength* of word you require, a thesaurus will damage your work rather than help it. To begin with, you may need to use a dictionary in harness with it – admittedly a slow and rather irksome task. But if you're prepared to endure a little toil at the outset, you'll find that the thesaurus soon becomes a valuable and speedy friend, and not the hidden trap it can be to the thoughtless, or rather non-thinking, user.

Successful use of dictionaries and thesauruses is as much a question of intelligence as of knowledge – in a way, more so. Knowledge is your *aim*: that aim cannot be achieved unless you apply your intelligence. Of course, someone else can tell you; but as Chris Pope pointed out in Chapter 9, someone else won't always be there when needed; and the sooner you apply your own thinking to the search for information, the happier and more efficient you'll be.

Other reference books
Use of these is less snag-ridden than dictionaries and thesauruses, especially if they have a good index. I find that most students experience problems not so much in using these books as in knowing which one to go to in the first place. There isn't, perhaps, much that a

book like this can do about such a problem: knowledge of the most suitable reference books for your particular purpose and subject is probably something you'll learn from your teacher and from the basic information included in your course. However, I can at least list a few admirable reference books that many students seem only vaguely aware of:

(1) *The Oxford 'Companion' series:* Covers a wide range of subjects. Entries are reliable, judicious and concise.
(2) *Oxford Specialist Dictionaries:* e.g. 'Etymology', 'Classical' and so on. Marvellous aids to the non-expert. Terminology and abbreviations take a while to become familiar, but information is clearly and helpfully set out.
(3) *Whitaker's Almanack:* A rich compendium of 'general' knowledge and information. It may seem eccentric if read through for any length of time – one jumps from anniversaries to maps to tide-times; but invaluable as a wide-ranging occasional helpmeet.
(4) *Fowler's English Usage:* Still the most authoritative guide to correct and elegant English.
(5) *Paperback Subject-Dictionaries:* There's a profusion of these around, of varying quality. In my own experience and opinion, Penguin take some beating: I have found their 'Art and Artists', 'Politics' and 'Geography' issues (all areas where I need a lot of help!) invaluable. By no means comprehensive, but excellent as 'ignition'.
(6) *Dictionary of National Biography:* Not only full of fascinating factual information, but of great additional interest to history, politics, literature and divinity students (especially) for the light it throws on the values and beliefs of the time of writing.

Productive use of reference books requires some understanding of how to use an index, which I go into shortly. As for how to find the right one for your needs at any given time: well, this will come in time, as you get used to using them and broadening your knowledge of them. In the meantime, teachers can help you, as can librarians (*q.v.*) and, perhaps most of all, fellow-students. Once you know, too, how to interpret and use a reading-list or a bibliography, your command and familiarity will soon grow. For there is one delightful bonus about using good reference books: not only do you find the specific information you're seeking, but you often learn or suddenly realize other things too. Thus regular and intelligent conference with such aids increases both your knowledge of valuable sources, and your knowledge and intelligence itself: you win on the swings *and* the roundabouts.

Libraries

A good library is a great deal more than a large collection of books and papers; and a librarian is much more than a person who stamps your books and bites into your loose change for late-return fines.

Nearly all Senior Librarians these days are highly trained graduates; and I have invariably found Chief Librarians to be extremely erudite, knowledgeable and, above all, friendly. I owe a good deal to the Chief Librarians of East Anglia and Sussex Universities, who found obscure, long-out-of-print books for me with remarkable speed and enthusiasm; and I have no doubt their counterparts elsewhere are no less admirable.

The aim of these remarks is not to offer a free commercial for librarians but to point out that, usually, they *like* to be asked to help you. Just like teachers, that is what they're paid for, and why they joined the profession in the first place. Nobody's going to die of excitement doing the obvious, mundane library chores; so a student with an interesting research request is invariably welcome. Even if they can't help you directly, they will almost certainly be able to point you in the right direction. These days, too, libraries are becoming more and more computerized – which, as my friend Christopher Turk shows in the next chapter, means that even a small-ish library has on tap staggering amounts of information.

So the first tip to any student for whom a library seems a rather forbidding, belittling place is: *they are there to help you.* As with teachers, never be afraid to ask.

Of course, you won't always *need* to ask. Any library will have a clear and comprehensive index system – both under author and subject. I go into indexes fully later; but most people, armed with either the name of the book or the author, should have no trouble finding out where the particular volume they need is located. It's also worth 'browsing' through a good index, just as one would in a bookshop (*q.v.*). Very often, you'll become aware not only of where the book you want is to be found, but of *other*, related books. These don't need to be read at once: simply to note them and thus add them to your over-all awareness of the field is itself useful. It was in just such a way, for example, that I first discovered that Henry Miller had not only written a number of outspoken novels, but a long essay on American life, *The Air Conditioned Nightmare*, which I would now say has some claim to be considered amongst his best work.

A library is also a rich storehouse of periodicals and academic papers, material that will eventually be important to any serious student. For remember: not all valuable work appears in books. Indeed, in some subjects – particularly science – it can be argued that, for a knowledge of the latest developments and thinking in a given area, periodicals and papers are more valuable than books. After all, a fair proportion of academic books comprise material first published in another form; in addition, a book, to be marketable, can't afford to be *too* far ahead of established thinking. Often an exciting new paper *changes* established thinking, almost overnight, and thus becomes a highly marketable force as a book (the wonderful work on DNA thirty years ago is a striking example). So browse among the periodicals, too: you'll be delighted to find out how much you pick up. More on this topic can be found shortly in the section on Periodicals.

Lastly, of course, libraries are proverbial as sanctums of quiet in which one can work uninterruptedly. Personally, as I hinted early on in the book, I do not find such an atmosphere conducive to my best work. But many do find it exactly what they want; and if this is true of you, then you're fortunate. For in that case your library can serve you simultaneously as a study, a vast resource, a pleasant place to browse, and a source of further enquiry. Perhaps best of all, most of them are free!

As I've mentioned, many new students find libraries somewhat awesome, scary places. And it's true that the experience of being dwarfed by hundreds of thousands of books can be unnerving: even now, after years of study, I still feel sharply aware, on entering a large library, of how enormous is the amount I don't know and haven't read. But although this is a natural and even salutory feeling, it doesn't do to allow it to possess you in a negative way. The pleasures of using a good library are many; and the advantages of learning how to use its multifarious resources cannot be overestimated. A library is every student's friend; and if you can cultivate that attitude early on, your student life will be much nicer.

Periodicals

I've already touched on why periodicals can be important and exciting sources of new information. But they have other uses as well.

To begin with, regular perusal of what I'll call the 'standard' weekly periodicals, e.g. *The Spectator, The Economist*, is both informative and enjoyable. The majority are very well written, and often highly entertaining as well as instructive. Such reading is just the thing for 'semiwork' – part of the 'ticking over' process I talk about in the first part of the book. In addition, some of these publications, e.g. *Private Eye* in the UK and *The Village Voice* in the USA, quite often print information or opinion rarely encountered elsewhere, and thus can be a major source of surprising and sardonic revelation.

The 'heavier' periodicals are, it's true, frequently less stylish or simply enjoyable, and may require early perseverance. But they are potentially very valuable indeed. Science students in particular should investigate as many relevant periodicals as they can; for, as I suggested when talking about libraries, the current pace of scientific discovery is such that often, by the time scientific work appears in book form, it is already partially out of date. This is particularly true at present of computer studies: the explosion of advances in that field means that most publications in it have to be substantially revised every year at the least. It thus makes sense to check out the new theories and studies as they first appear. Your teachers should be conversant with the periodicals that will be most use to you, and your library staff can also assist.

Humanities students are hardly less advantaged by regular acquaintance with their fields' leading periodicals. The transformation in historical studies in schools over the last fifteen years (use of original documents and so on) was engendered through articles and debates in historical journals; and in my own field, literature, it is no accident that the two most significant 'movements' – Practical Criticism and Structuralism – both acquired their initial impact in periodical essays.

Of course, there *are* rather a lot of the damned things! And a new student may feel somewhat overwhelmed by such volume, and feel helpless as to where to start and which ones to trust most. Once again, this will solve itself in time. You will become aware of which journals best satisfy your requirements or your tastes. As with most other study matters, a combination of honesty with yourself and belief in your own instincts will get you over those first hurdles, and soon, I can assure you, regular reading of a specialist periodical or two will be a normal and pleasurable part of your academic diet.

One last thing about periodicals. Nearly all of them operate on a tight financial margin; and this means that they depend on advertising to break even. Accordingly, a specialist periodical will carry a lot of information in the advertisements themselves – news of new books, new equipment, new ideas. Such a valuable source of information – including things you might not see mentioned elsewhere – is yet another reason why the committed student should cultivate a familiarity with the leading periodicals in his field. Like libraries, they may at first seem dry and forbidding, but will richly reward the student who is determined to make the best use of them.

The interpretation of reading-lists

The biggest problem for a student about any reading-list is that he's dependent upon the competence of whoever devised it. I don't simply mean the deviser's knowledge of the field and of the books he cites: we can, I hope, take that for granted. But a good reading-list should, I think, include a comment or two about the particular nature and quality of each book. If this is the case, then you probably don't need much extra advice from me.

If, however, your reading-list is simply an unannotated roll of titles and authors, then you can help yourself in a number of useful ways. First, try to determine which are 'primary' works, and which are 'secondary'. This distinction is quite simple in the humanities: a primary work in history is a source written at the time, or in literature a play or work of fiction, while the secondary material is that which comments upon and analyses that primary work. In Science, and subjects like Economics and Geography, the difference is perhaps less easy to determine, since most work in these areas simultaneously *combines* creative discovery and analysis. In these subjects, therefore, it may take longer to establish which texts are essentially primary, and those that are predominantly secondary. But it should eventually become clear enough for you to make a sensible start on covering the list.

Once you have a reasonable idea which of the two categories the books come under, I think it's best to start with one or two primary texts, in order to acquaint yourself with the basic material. You *can*, it's true, pick up a lot of information from secondary sources without first so much as looking at primary material; but it's dangerous. There are times when, like most people, I've bluffed my way through a discussion about something I haven't read or seen by relying on secondhand information; but I've found, often very embarrassingly, that it's only a matter of time before the full extent of my underlying ignorance is devastatingly revealed! It is also a *slower* method, even if it seems gentler and more convenient at the time.

Another simple aid you can employ is just to note *frequency* of appearance of authors or concepts. If, for example, an author is cited three or four times, it's safe to assume that he's important to your study, and you could do worse than start with his work. In addition, it's worth taking the trouble to find out what else he's written that's *not* mentioned on the list. Similarly, if the same phrase or idea occurs in several of the titles, you can assume it's central to the knowledge you're being asked to acquire; so that's another useful place to begin.

If your list is not very helpful, however, you may have to seek further advice from whoever designed it. This will need a little tact, but is worth while. Reading-lists can be very forbidding, almost hostile, documents; and a chat with your teacher is likely to establish a greater sense of comfort about the whole thing. You will probably learn, for example, that much of the list is *not* essential, but is recommended for your further interest and growth. This doesn't mean you should ignore such books; but it does mean you don't religiously have to cover each one in sequence to stay on course. A reading-list is advice, not a command. Dip into it if you like (using the kind of methods I outline in Chapter 6), and find out which writers you find most stimulating and useful. If you're not reading enough, you'll soon be told, or it will become evident in other ways.

Finally, annotate and revise your reading-list yourself. Over the year or whatever, other books will be recommended, or you'll read them independently; and it's a good idea to relate them in some way to the original list. In this way, you can use your list *critically*, and thus incorporate it creatively into your other course work.

Bookshops

Much the same is true of bookshops as is true of libraries; but there are one or two additional points worth making.

The best thing about bookshops these days is that they too have been caught up in the computer revolution. As a result, even a small book-shop in, say, a market town, will have available a complete record of books in print, plus information about titles that are being reprinted and when they'll be available. This is not only a valuable information service: in my experience, it means that books can be ordered for you more quickly than used to be the case.

The major benefit of this advance is that it has transformed bookshop assistants into instant mines of information. Gone are the days when it was possible to meet staggering ignorance in the most famous bookshops in the country (I'll never forget asking, as an undergraduate, for a copy of *Piers Plowman* – a set text for over four hundred Cambridge students – and being asked in return, 'Which of his books did you want, sir?'!). An enquiry will be answered with comprehensive accuracy within a few minutes: I've even known bookshops work out from my muddled, half-digested snippets of information which book I'm talking about, and where I can get it most quickly.

Bookshops are, in any event, pleasant places to spend time. No-one minds you browsing (most shops encourage it), and it's thus a good place to dip into books and start your knowledge of them, even if it's months before you get round to buying and reading them. And a last word on second-hand bookshops: it really is amazing what you can pick up. Forgotten but good essays on an area in your field not only make fascinating reading: they increase your sense of the development and changes in that field, which can only be good for your study and its own development.

Abstracts and indexes

An abstract is a short summary of a work or an argument (usually in thesis form, or something similar). They are extremely useful for anyone seeking particular information on a topic, for they take very little time to read, and announce their main direction and conclusions clearly and without fuss. All universities carry a facility known as Dissertations Abstracts (DA): they used to be printed in the form of telephone directories, but are now computerized, and collected on easy-to-use sheets. And although it's unlikely that a new student will need to refer to such material at first, there will come a time when your own knowledge is extensive and sophisticated enough for such research to be both useful and stimulating. Incidentally, it is often worth while, if only as a brief mental exercise, to concoct abstracts of your own work, or of stuff you have read. I talk further about this in the next section.

Using an index productively is more of a skill than might be imagined. Obviously, any old fool can look up, say, 'President Nixon' in the index to a book on US politics, and establish where he is mentioned, or perhaps analysed in detail. But, rather like a reading-list, you are at the mercy of the compiler. Many indexes are by no means comprehensive: they simply list the major topics and names covered – and this may mean that the precise thing you're after is not mentioned. If this happens, it's unwise to assume at once that the book doesn't contain what you want. Try another 'heading', or even a third, before you move on to the next possible source.

Let's take an example, developing one I've just hinted at. Let us suppose you are researching the Watergate scandal in America in the early 'seventies. You look up 'Watergate' in the index, and find to your dismay that it's only mentioned once. 'Not much use,' you say to yourself, and prepare to find another book instead. But wait. Maybe there *is* a lot of valuable material about the scandal in the book you're about to discard. Try looking under 'President Nixon'. Or under 'John Dean' (centrally involved in the whole business). You might even try under '1972 Presidential Election' (which took place just after the original Watergate burglary, from which the whole scandal snow-balled). In other words, don't give up on a book until you've checked out all the information you've got against the index.

You see, by the time you're *ready* to use an index, you'll know a fair bit about what you want to further your knowledge in. People who know nothing about a subject don't start by using the index: there's no point, because it won't mean anything to them. They'll have to read up about the subject a bit before they're in a position to narrow their focus of enquiry in such a way. So when consulting an index, stay aware of *all* the information you've got. If, to take another example, you're working on Scott Fitzgerald, don't just try his name, but also 'American Novelists'; 'Hollywood'; his various book-titles; even 'alcoholism'. I think you'll be surprised by how often the second or even the third entry that you consult turns out to be very profitable, when the apparently most obvious, first choice disappointed.

Indexes are also very useful tools for rapid cross-reference. To return to our example of 'President Nixon': most books about US politics of the 'sixties and early 'seventies will have masses of material about him; and this will be reflected in the gigantic index-entry under his name. If you're researching just one aspect of his career and administration, you'll need to check out other places in the index, and establish a clear 'fix' on which part of the book has what you really want. This method is analogous to direction-finding using three bearings, used to establish a precise location for a plane, a transmitter, or something more mundane like a church steeple or bench mark.

Sometimes, using an index can give you an early sense of whether the book is going to be reliable or not. To take a faintly ludicrous example: if you pick up a book entitled, say, *Great English Painters*, and the index contains no mention of Constable and only one reference to Turner, you can be pretty sure that the book is, at the very least, eccentric, if not positively ignorant or deranged. And such short-cuts are perfectly legitimate, sensible methods of coping with the vast amounts of potential reading available to you. An index, intelligently read, can do very similar work to an abstract: it can establish clearly and revealingly what the author's major preoccupations are, and from that it may well be possible to work out his over-all point of view. Try out the index in this book, and see if I'm right!

Personal indexes

As I've stressed from the start of this book, there are as many ways of working successfully as there are students who succeed; so there is no need to feel that you *must* adopt some kind of 'personal index' system. To be perfectly frank, I don't use one myself: my mind works in other ways, and finds other methods quicker and more convenient, so I've never persevered with constructing one – there's never been any point. But I do know many students and colleagues who find an index-system immensely time-saving and helpful to them; so here are a few basic tips about how to go about establishing one.

As with mnemonics (see Chapters 4 and 7), the *precise* format and method is entirely up to you, for you know your own rhythms and organizatory methods best. The most obvious over-all method might seem to be alphabetical; but you might find you'd rather do it under topics-headings, or something else. Quite a lot will depend on what subject you're indexing. If it's history, a chronological approach might suit you best, whereas this method is unlikely to be a great help in literature or physics, say.

Although I don't use an index system in my work, I do in my hobby (more a passion, in fact), which is collecting records, mainly jazz. I have in the past used an alphabetical system throughout; but at present I file my classical records according to chronology, and my jazz LPs under broad stylistic headings, or according to instrument. This has a drawback, in that nobody else in the family knows where to find a given record! But at least *I* know; and that, as with you and your study method, is the real point.

It's a matter of taste and temperament how large and inclusive you wish to make any such system. Some people just log important references (books and page-numbers, etc.) that they know they'll want to find quickly and regularly; others extend their system to include summaries of their own essays, listed both chronologically and cross-referring to other, similar work done at another time. Such an advanced system takes time to compile – especially if you're starting from scratch. But if you find it tolerably enjoyable, it can be very valuable, for two distinct reasons. Firstly, once you've done it, you'll have a strongly organized, personally logical resource centre that is all your own, and you will rarely have to waste time hunting feverishly for something you know you've read/written but have forgotten where it is. And secondly, the very *act* of going over all your work and rearranging it into a new reference system is a kind of intensive revision which will reinforce and probably clarify your knowledge. Even better, the process of systematizing it all may well make you aware of connections that you hadn't thought of before, thus broadening and sharpening your knowledge all round.

In sum: you can use a personal index in any way you like, and include in it as much or as little as you wish. As I say, not everyone will want to make such a system a part of their study-organization; but for those whom it suits, it can be a great technical aid and also a considerable boost to confidence and sense of security. If you're one of the fast-growing army of people who have some kind of personal computer, then you'll have a lot of fun using it for such a purpose (for which a computer is absolutely tailor-made, by the way). The nice thing about them all, however, be they computerized or 'longhand', is that you, and only you, are in charge; and the construction of an efficient and time-saving index system is one of the best ways I've encountered of convincing an individual student that he has talent and an independent mind.

Conclusion

If the information revolution of our time means anything profound (beyond, that is, the creation of a new technology and a shift in employment patterns), it is that students and academics of the future are going to be less crucially at the mercy of their memories. This does not, I hope, mean that my earlier chapters on Memory are about to become redundant! But it is probably true that great success for a future student will depend rather less than at present on his having a super-power memory. Just as important are going to be good organization and an efficient working knowledge of sources and resources. I seem to have quoted Dr Johnson a good deal during this book; but once again a remark of his is most apposite:

'Knowledge is of two kinds. We know a subject ourselves, or we know where we can find information upon it.'

I hope this brief introduction to how and where to find information has helped to start you off, and that you can now see that there is no need to be frightened of the new technology that impinges upon study, or of the size and wealth of the various storehouses. They are all there to help you, and you can be assured of a welcome.

A PERSONAL COMPUTER TO SAVE YOUR SWEAT

David Kelly

There are two types of computer people. Those with heads buzzing with the numbers of machine-code Peeks and Pokes. And those who find the whole subject so unbelievably boring it is beneath them to get involved. One notch under joining the college model railway society.

To the latter group – who I guess are in the majority – the personal computer or home micro does little except keep the proponents of global thermonuclear war out of harm's way, tucked up in their Hall of Residence playing *Mutant Camels Battle at the End of Time*.

They are wrong. It will be hard to escape the implications of microchip technology in your college studies regardless of what course you are taking and your own computer could possibly save you an awful lot of sweat over the years.

It is important to realize what a microcomputer can be useful for – and where its use would be inappropriate. For example, a micro *can* give – without a second's thought – spreadsheet financial modelling with built-in inflation accounting and look-up tax tables. But even those on a minimum grant will find that the back of an old envelope still wins hands down.

So what can it *usefully* do? It can be used to make sure that any written work to be handed in and assessed is perfectly typed, and smartly presented – word processing. It will manipulate any amount of data and draw conclusions from it; either in the form of graphs produced from figures – graphics packages; or in the form of conclusions from word responses, say from a questionnaire, which can be easily collated – database programs.

When finals loom near it can be used to test the effectiveness of your revision. And it can be used for relaxation – perhaps for a game of chess; or to compose another song for the band.

A crucial fact is that all this can be accomplished without knowing how to program. For most machines it is possible to buy ready-written software which can be simply adapted to match your requirements.

Computers are not cheap – you will have to convince yourself that it really will be of use to you. Not far off, though, is the time when every college student will be required to have a microcomputer as a matter of course. This is already happening in America, where several universities have supplied each of their students with a micro completely free. I wouldn't hold your breath for that to happen here!

As you would expect, you get what you pay for. Prices are still falling fast so it is difficult to be firm about the cost. A minimum system of a small computer and printer could cost as little as £250. A more complex arrangement with everything you always wanted but were afraid to indulge in would be nearer £500.

The sort of things to look for when buying a computer are:

Memory – the machine should have enough memory – called RAM – to store at least a few pages of text at a time. Memory prices are dropping so new machines will offer more for your money. Anything less than 48K RAM is probably not worth while.

Keyboard – a proper typewriter-feel keyboard is better than the rubber-key type or calculator-style buttons. Make sure the keyboard is full size. Some of them are subtly smaller and the closer key spacing makes reliable typing more difficult.

Processor – the 'brains' of the computer – varies from machine to machine. Most of the present micros use what are called 8-bit processors. Machines are beginning to appear which are either 16- or 32-bit. They are faster.

Software – for the majority of us who cannot program to save our lives software is crucial. Any machine is only as good as the software that is available for it. Software is not easily transferrable from one machine to another. Some machines which look promising at first glance have next to no software written for them. Instead of a good buy they are goodbye to several hundred quid.

Printers – having composed your epic novel on the computer you will want to print it out. You will want a plain-paper printer rather than one of the types that print on funny heat-sensitive or metallized sheets. There are two main sorts. Dot-matrix printers are cheaper – around £100. They produce the kind of printing you get on letters from the bank. Each character is made up of an arrangement of dots. More expensive is a daisy-wheel printer. For around £250 you get a machine that gives results like an expensive typewriter using a ribbon.

Storage – having written your document or organized your data you will want to store it. The cheapest method is to store it on cassette. The major disadvantages of this method are speed – it is painfully slow;

capacity – less than other methods; and it is unreliable – you end up fiddling about with volume and recording levels all the time.

Another point: some computers will not work with an ordinary cassette player and need a special one. A better system is the 'stringy floppy', a high-speed tape loop. The method is a lot faster but still leaves something to be desired as far as reliability is concerned. Finally, there are floppy disc storage devices. These are by far the best but also the most expensive. Costing around £250 they come in different sizes and capacities. Both 3 inch and 3½ inch discs are becoming more popular than the more traditional 5-inch ones. They come in single- or double-sided and single- and double-density versions. It is the *formatted* capacity that is the measure of its amount of storage.

Display – home micros do not have built-in displays. So you will need a TV, either a second-hand black-and-white or a sparkling new colour one – your choice. Alternatively, you can go for a top-quality picture by buying a monitor at around £400!

Now let's see what a microcomputer can do.

Word-processing is just like typing, only better. The best are the 'what you see is what you get' sort. You see on the TV screen what you have typed out in the form that it will be when you instruct the computer to print it. Unlike a typewriter it is very flexible. You can edit at will, adding in words and deleting others. Text automatically carries over to the next line. You set the margins and the page size. Most word-processors keep a built-in word, line and page count. Using a moving pointer – called the cursor – you can go back over what you have already written and make changes to it, swapping one sentence for another or changing a phrase. Having written a piece you can move paragraphs around, changing their order if you want. Text is automatically justified. Most word-processors will print in various styles – bold, italic, underlined. Some will store useful phrases, chosen by the writer, so that they can be recalled by pressing only one key.

The outstanding advantage of a computer with word-processing software is that you can get your project report or essay just right before automatically printing it out. If you spot an amazing error when reading it through afterwards you don't have to type it all out again. Simply reload the tape or disc into the computer, make your changes, and give the machine the print command again. Invaluable.

The applications of a database are less easy to explain because they are more various. A database program is like a box of index cards. Each card is a screen-full of information, and you can type onto the screens and flip through them at will. The strength of a database over a card index is that the computer knows what is on each card and can search them more efficiently and in more complex ways than you ever could. Anything from the results of a questionnaire to paragraphs from Shakespeare plays could be stored. From these you can direct it to search for applicants who smoke more than 10 cigarettes a day, rats which keeled over after a certain dose rate, or references to the word 'death' in *Macbeth*. At a more sophisticated level, most databases will search files for entries that satisfy more than one criterion. For example, you could enter data on the countries of the world and get the computer to select those countries with population over a certain level where French was a commonly spoken language.

A database is very much what you make of it. It can be a waste of time. Or it can make it easy to draw some revealing conclusions from a confusing sea of information. Among its other uses could be applications like keeping records of friends' addresses and birthdays!

Some graphics packages now being sold can be used to relieve, instantly, hours of painstaking plotting. You can input raw figures and immediately get line-graphs, curves or pie-charts. More interestingly, you can take sets of graphs and change them mathematically – say by subtracting one graph from another. Such operations become as easy as pressing a few keys so it becomes simple just to play around with your figures just to see what turns up.

A microcomputer can be invaluable at revision time. There are any number of programs to test French language vocabularies or atomic structures. The best are programs where you can set your own questions and answers. Just trying to sort out which problems to set yourself and their answers is as good a way of revising as any other. There are also some quite useful literature programs around dealing with specific plays and novels and work on roughly the same principle.

Finally, recreation. Your computer need not switch off when you do. Some of the software titles around will give you a pretty good game of chess. Or Scrabble or backgammon or poker (although it must be admitted that playing poker against the computer is not quite the same as the real thing!).

Many home computers have built-in music synthesizers. They can be connected to a full-size music keyboard allowing you to experiment with writing different tunes and then storing them away for future use.

There are any number of interests for which a computer can be very helpful. Amateur radio is a good example. The micro can be used to encode and automatically decode morse. If you are involved with the organization of any college society then a computer could be used to keep membership lists, print out mailing-addresses, work out the team's performance over the season and so on.

And of course there are games to be played and adventures to be had. You too can find yourself stuck in *The Hobbit* wandering for ever through the Elven King's Halls.

12
• • • • •
Computers and study*

Christopher Turk

You are likely to be asking, 'Why a chapter on computers in a book about study?' Those of you interested in computers will probably read it anyway. Those of you bored, frightened, or simply not interested, will skip it. But don't skip it. I'm not writing about coloured boxes with flashing lights in a kind of *Playschool* 'Coo! Look what it can do!' spirit. Nor am I going to deal with crude, bleeping representations of klingons, and horrific mass-killings in a mindless blitzkrieg world. Computers are rather more important than that, now.

Why are computers important to the student? Let me suggest tl:ree reasons, and then go on to deal with them in turn.

Firstly, there is a type of computer called a word-processor; and word-processing saves a very large amount of time, produces impressively neat and well-organized documents, and your competitors are already using them. Secondly, you are going to need to know about computers, because libraries and all sorts of information-sources are using them more and more. Thirdly, it has been said – rightly, I think – that the most interesting thing about computers is the way they illustrate how our *own* brains work. This area, known as Cognitive Science, is as important as Galileo was for Donne, or Newton was for Hume. It's going to change the humanities.

I hope that I have grabbed your attention, so let me launch into the first of these three topics, word-processing. There was a time when word-processors were used to write thousands of identical letters from credit-card companies, and for not much else. Then trendy writers (such as Jeffrey Archer and John le Carré – if they will forgive me) used them. Now a rising proportion of books, theses and essays are being

---

* This chapter is primarily intended for humanities students.

produced on them. Many postgraduates use them, quite a few under-graduates write their essays on them, and before you know it sixth-form essays will be appearing neatly typed, beautifully formatted, all corrections included, and impeccably revised.

I know a very nice lady, who uses her leisure to write charming stories for six-year-olds. She was recently asked by her husband if he could spend some of the family budget on a home computer. Although mystified, she is of a kindly disposition, and graciously consented. Last time we visited her, she took my six-year-old to the study, and the buzz of a computer-printer started. My daughter came out delighted, clutching a story which had been freshly typed for her. And what a good story too! My nice, and not very young, lady had learnt word-processing in no time.

The point is that it's not difficult to learn to use a word-processor. And with one you can add, change, and rewrite at will, and what comes out is still perfectly neat and tidy.

I'm not saying that all essays must be done on a word-processor, any more than that all essays must be typed. Neat hand-writing is still impressive. But for the special piece of work, the prize essay, the dissertation, and eventually (as your skills develop) the regular weekly essay, the word-processor will replace the typewriter as the thing to use.

Word-processors are not a great deal more expensive than type-writers. A good electric typewriter costs £400, and a word-processor can now be had from £1000 upwards. At present, only those who already have a home computer, or have access to the school/college computer, are likely to be word-processing. But prices are dropping, and soon anyone who five years ago would have had a typewriter will have a word-processor.

What can they do for us? I like to divide their advantages into three: they change the *psychology* of creating a document; they ease the *burden* of inserting and checking references; and they *encourage* revision of style, structure and content.

Firstly, then, the psychology of writing. One of the commonest mistakes an inexperienced writer makes is to think a document should always be written from the beginning forwards. The novice writer sits down with a blank sheet of paper, and a pen, and tries to write the first sentence. He can't, of course, because he hasn't thought through what he's doing. It's like setting off on a journey without first deciding where to go. Or rather, it's like starting to make a meal by sitting down in front of an empty plate, with a knife and fork in your hands. Dishing-up is the last stage of cooking a meal. And sitting down with blank paper should be the last stage of writing.

Everyone is familiar with the teacher's regular exhortations to make a plan first. The good student has even found that it really does pay, and does it. You can't write a document unless you have some idea of what points you are going to make, the ground you hope to cover, and the conclusions you are going to draw. In the past, it was necessary to take a sheet of paper, and scribble a plan, notes of a few paragraphs, and a few ideas. As these ideas developed more notes were added, squeezing themselves into corners. Then you had to start a new sheet, and references such as 'add from (A)' crept in. Eventually, one started writing using what looked like a piece of knitting as a guide.

I said 'in the past' because word-processors change all that. The main reason for the change is that words on a screen can be moved around easily. You can insert as much as you like, where you like. You can also change the position of various bits of text. Best of all, you can print a fresh copy of your draft, take it away with a cup of coffee, and see what it feels like to read. You can scribble notes, draw arrows, and experiment with new arrangements on the draft. The text on the machine can then be altered, and another draft printed. You can then see what the new revised arrangement looks like. And alter it again if you need to.

What I am saying is that word-processors transform the task of structuring a document; and they therefore transform the *techniques* of creating it. I now start all my writing by jotting down (on the word-processor) a few general key words for topics I need to cover. Next I open up space between the headings, and draft a bit of text. When I have new information, new ideas, or simply new energy, I go back and add more text where it's appropriate. I often add a few notes in one place, and leave them to be filled out later. The planning and drafting stages now go hand in hand, and the text grows by a sort of internal ferment.

Experts in the psychology of writing have always recommended the writer to start in the middle of his text.* Start writing what is most familiar and comfortable, and leave the difficult bits – especially the conclusions and the introduction – until later. (How, anyway, can you introduce something you don't yet know?!) Word-processors turn the ideal into easy reality. Using one, you are able to let your document grow by a natural, organic process of thought. I suppose it's the

---

* See pages 91 ff. Indeed, all of Chapter 8 confirms and amplifies the arguments here.

knowledge that I can easily alter and improve my writing which helps me to bang away on the keyboard without feeling any of the old worries or constraints. It was the sheer labour of typing and retyping a draft that made most writing so poor. Now the retyping can be done at speed by a machine, the writer feels far less exhausted at the *prospect* of redrafting, and the result is thus much better.

It has already been pointed out to you in this book that many human thought-processes are not linear. We all know that our minds work in a spreading pattern, not in a straight line. The creation of documents on a word-processor follows the spreading pattern, not the linear one. The great constraint language imposes is that its movement is linear, while ideas often describe a circular motion. The task of putting ideas down in prose is very largely the task of choosing an appropriate order. Word-processors make this easier.

The second advantage I cited, you may remember, was easing the burden on the writer. A word-processor does this by removing the need to be over-concerned about details while writing. If you stop to check a date, find and insert a quotation, look up a spelling, or just to wrestle with the syntax of a python-like sentence, the flow of your thoughts will be broken. That complex of ideas, carefully juggled and held in suspense in your mind while the words flow out, will be spoiled, even temporarily lost. With the word-processor, you can insert a mere guess, or a star (*) where you're not sure, and go straight on. (Admittedly, you can do this under other methods and systems: my point is that a word-processor actively *encourages* you to do so.) When you're tired of being creative, or when nothing seems to be able to get your mind going, you can go back over the writing, picking out the references to be checked, the spelling to be looked up, and the sentences to be wrestled with. Dealt with one by one they seem minor tasks; and this not only makes the business more congenial, but is a first-class way of igniting your mind for further *major* work – which, as Chapter 2 demonstrated, is often the hardest part of any student's life.

So if you train yourself to keep going – and the word-processor greatly facilitates this – your writing will flow better. Such removal of extra pressure is one thing I mean by reducing the burden. The other is a simple physical thing. When you've inserted your quotations, checked the dates/formulae, looked up and added the references, and corrected the grammar, you don't need laboriously to retype the final copy. This was the job which many writers did in the small hours of the morning, just before the document was due. Now no longer. The machine will retype, it will do it a hundred times faster than you can, and it won't make any *more* mistakes while it does so. Word-processors lighten the burden on the fingers as well as the mind – and they leave you more time to do something else more productive and enjoyable.

The third of the three advantages is that, as I've already suggested, they *encourage* revision. By this I don't mean just spelling and grammar: I mean the habit of mind which, instead of worshipping every word which slips from your pen, critically and judiciously examines every sentence for flab, every word for laxity and rightness. I like Dr Johnson's advice: 'Read over your compositions, and wherever you meet with a passage which you think is particularly fine, *strike it out*.'

A word of warning which endorses what Richard Palmer and Chris Pope have recommended at earlier times in this book: avoid revising your work straight after writing it. Absence makes the writer grow sounder, and physical dividers should be used to distance you a little from what you've just written. Best of all is next morning, or even after a good weekend away. If not that, then at least a meal should separate revision from writing. When you come back to what you've written, you are more nearly in the position of the reader. You can see if you've actually said what you meant.

The habit of looking at your own writing with a foreign eye is an excellent one. Practice improves it. You learn to suspect sentences which go on for several lines, and it soon becomes easy to chop them in two. You become suspicious of the flowery word, you grow adept at smelling out a cliché, and you often, while mulling over what you've written, suddenly discover just the word that gives biting edge. I find the best results of revision are pithy three- or four-word sentences, and portly pairs of adjectives reduced to a slim-line image. W. B. Yeats was the most assiduous reviser: his manuscripts show him choosing new words, crossing them out and choosing again, trying another, and going to and fro between phrases until he has achieved exactly the effect he wants. It shows in his poetry. Not in the way the naïve writer might predict, with seams and gaps everywhere, but with a naturalness and rightness to every word which is matchless.

Word-processors, then, can transform the task of writing. You are not obliged to rush out and buy one; and at present you can't use them in exams. But if you do have access to one, I counsel you to start learning. People who use them produce much more impressive writing. Besides, they are *fun*, almost like toys in terms of the fascinating pleasure they can give. And as has been stressed throughout this book, the more fun you can derive from your study, the more successful you are likely to be.

The second justification for this chapter was that computers are increasingly being used as research tools. Patrick Winston has written of his research: 'the central goals . . . are to make computers more useful, and to understand the principles which make intelligence possible'.* I want to deal with both these aims as the second and third of my reasons why computers are useful to students.

Computers are useful research tools. They have been used in science and maths research for several decades, and are now coming into their own as aids in humanities research. Students will soon be used to seeing terminals (VDUs or Visual Display Units – basically TV screens with typewriter-like keyboards) in libraries. As I write, workmen in the corridor outside my office are putting in cables to run a terminal from the computer to our library. From it students will be able to search through the full records of our own, and other, libraries. They will be able to locate a book they need, and identify new books in their subject. Previously this could be done with a card index, a note-pad, and a lot of time. The computer makes it both quicker and more thorough. Computers work very fast – something like four million individual operations per second is typical. It takes a great number of these individual operations to make up a book search, but even so the speed is impressive. Computers are also thorough. The old jokes about astronomical gas-bills were the fault of the programmers, not the computer. Computers double check every fragment of information they handle, and the actual error rate is minuscule – something like one garbled letter every few hundred books checked would be about par. So with a computer library index, you can find books both quickly and reliably.

Such increased speed is obviously a large bonus when tracking down books you know about. But the great advantage of computers is their ability to locate books you *didn't* know about. They can give you the reference to any book which mentions the subject you want in its title, and also any book which mentions a name as author, editor, or subject. They can additionally combine these names and subjects.

These methods for searching a big library catalogue are well established, and the next few years should see a more human face put on them. They will become easier to understand (the basic principle is a starkly obvious logic) and therefore more widely used. Two developments (amongst many) will give you some idea of future progress. Firstly, the ability to search very large catalogues very quickly – at the rate of something like 150 000 words per second! – is a rate of research

*Winston, P. H. (1974) *Artificial Intelligence*, Addison-Wesley, p. 1.

likely to transform much traditional painstaking scholarship. Secondly, it is now possible to search distant library catalogues. The British Library has a system called BLAISE, which enables you to search through all the library's catalogues from a terminal in your own library. It can also search the American Library of Congress catalogue, which is updated using a satellite. Using BLAISE, I can search the major American and British collections from my desk, using the same terminal I am writing these words on.

Amongst other things computers can now do for the humanities is the availability of much cheaper and better printing for both text and music, using a laser-typesetter. This means that a lot of scholarly work, which was uneconomical before, can now be published. Computers can also do simple scholarly tasks, such as constructing word-lists and concordances of literary works, or making very accurate deductions about the authorship of a piece of writing. This can help solve scholarly puzzles, such as who wrote Shakespeare or the Gospels. You may find this uninteresting, and it is certainly intellectually trivial. But accuracy has always been the foundation of good scholarship, and to know something for certain makes literary judgements more reliable.

Computers, then, are useful to the scholar, and are not just for gas-bills and bank accounts. They will read, digest, and make judgements about larger bodies of work than a human scholar could cover in several lifetimes. They will help him write his books and articles, and print them quickly and cheaply. These alone are good reasons for scholars to love computers. Don't be frightened of the air-conditioned boxes, or the jargon. Most of us who use computers for humanities research never see the beast itself. It lurks in a separate room, and all we have is a neat screen, with black letters on a white background, and a small keyboard. It's no more frightening than a typewriter. I am quite sure that a computer is easier to use than a car: for one thing, your mistakes don't hurt so much!

The third reason why computers should interest students, and the second aim Winston gave, is that they provide new ways of understanding our own brains. Much of this book has been about how to use your brain – a lot of time has been spent describing how the brain works, and giving advice on how to drive this awesome machine to your best advantage. Artificial Intelligence (AI), or the attempt to make computers do things which would be regarded as intelligent if done by a human being, has resulted in a wealth of fascinating new insights into the human brain.

To begin with, in order to be truly intelligent computers need to be able to see, and to speak. Seeing is something we humans take for granted, but it has become clear that a great deal of processing has to be done before we can 'see' the object. Nevertheless, the whole process of focusing, interpreting depth and shape, and then identifying an object as a cow/a chair/whatever, is quite automatic. Attempting to make computers do this has made us realize what an enormous amount of processing, and what a large part of the brain, is involved. Yet human beings are completely unaware of what goes on. Some body functions, like breathing or heart-beat, can be brought into our consciousness. Other functions, such as digestion or sweating, cannot be controlled, but we are well aware of their effects. But most of the brain's functions lie outside our awareness: we apparently know very little about the mechanism we use all day.

The same is true of language. We have no access to the rules by which we form a sentence, though rules there must be, because we know when one is wrong. Nor can we find the mechanisms which give meanings to words, or make poetry moving. We can, rather shakily, deduce what these rules might be. But they are not conscious. The attempt to make computers talk is one of the most interesting areas of research at the moment; and it is as much humanities research as science research. Language has always been the tool of the arts, and research in this area seems to be a real opportunity to close the great divide between arts and sciences.

The key to this exciting area is the uniquely human characteristic of self-awareness. We can all think; we can all make ourselves aware of ourselves thinking; and the further ability to reflect on that awareness is the quintessence of philosophy. Ever since Plato, all philosophers have addressed the phenomenon of the reflective nature of consciousness, or the ability to turn in on itself. Consciousness, it seems, is the centre of humanness.

It also emerges that the growth of consciousness is the core of progress through evolution. From plants with no central nervous system to animals aware of the world but little aware of themselves, earth has progressed to *Homo sapiens*, a species unique so far in its capacity for self-awareness. This awareness has grown staggeringly fast over the last few thousand years: through science, philosophy and culture, we are rapidly learning to control, understand and manipulate ourselves and the world we inhabit.

Nevertheless, human intelligence – substantially the highest evolutionary layer so far – has limitations. First, knowledge and experience take many, many years of education to develop in any one person. Education is a major task, as you know only too well! And all too soon after full intellectual maturity is reached, the arteries start hardening, the person retires, and dies. The techniques for preserving the contents of the educated and experienced mind before death are primitive. We use shaky summaries on pieces of boiled trees (which is all, let's face it, that paper actually is). It takes almost as long to read the information back into another still-working brain, and the error rate is high.

It is the inadequacy of this support system for human knowledge that has probably held down the take-off of technology. But now – that is, within a few, foreseeable, hundred years – it looks as if intelligence may be able to leave the biological systems which evolved it, and transfer to systems where growth will be sustained. Evolution has already reached the stage of self-aware intelligence; the next stage seems to be a further development in the ability of life-forms to be self-aware. And by 'life-forms' I include artificial, *built* systems – such as computers.

There is neither time nor space to go further into this huge area. Nor, perhaps, is it appropriate to do so in a book designed to aid the student in the 1980s. But I trust I'm not alone in finding it a thrilling prospect, and one which will exercise our minds from now on. Indeed, as I stated at the outset, I believe AI will be as important for our future culture as Galileo was for the Elizabethans, or Newton was for the Enlightenment.

However, there's no need for me to make such enormous claims to convince you, I hope, that computers are a fruitful subject for any student to contemplate. They can help you write essays and theses, they can help you do research, and they will gradually change the world of ideas we live and work in, just as Darwin's discoveries changed the world. Don't ignore computers.

● ● ● ● ● ● ● ● ● ● ●

PART 3

Examination: psychology and techniques

● ● ● ● ● ● ● ● ● ● ●

Examinations are a built-in part of nearly all vocational courses. The overwhelming likelihood, therefore, is that you will face an exam at the end of your course – be it after one, two or three years. And no book on study would be complete without a chapter investigating their purpose, the attitudes they inspire, and the techniques that can help you to succeed at them.

Teachers dislike exams too

The first point to make is that nearly all students dislike exams. Indeed, student unease about them is far and away the greatest and most frequent problem that teachers encounter amongst their classes. As a result, a lot of *teachers* dislike exams too. They feel under pressure on their own account (since results reflect nearly as much on them as on the students themselves), and they become disturbed and positively protective about the intensity with which some of their students worry. This can create a vicious circle, whereby teacher and student simply aggravate each other's suspicions and fear.

Chris Pope and I hope that the following sections will help you to relax somewhat about exams, and lead you to regarding them as just another part of the course rather than as a horrific and undermining ordeal. You may be interested, even comforted, to learn that he and I are not fully in accord about exams: he loathes them, while I (with a less impressive track record than his, sparing his blushes) always enjoyed them as a student, and still consider them valuable and legitimate. Both of us are agreed, however, that taking exams is a *skill*. The activity is not a lottery, an arbitrary, Act-of-God-type happening, or an evil game run by a secret society. It is a perfectly rational method of assessment whose techniques can be comfortably mastered. As with any skill, you have to possess some aptitude, and work at it. There can be little doubt that you have the aptitude – after all, if you didn't, you probably wouldn't have lasted the course long enough to get anywhere near the exam. The application, as always, is up to you; but we hope that the discussion and advice that follow will make such work both worth while and agreeable.

13

• • • • •

Examinations: psychology and attitudes

Everything in life, including marriage, is done under pressure.

Isaiah Berlin

Objections to exams

If I asked you to summarize your objections to exams, I imagine you would arrive at a list that approximates this one:

(1) Exams put an excessive premium on speed.

(2) That accent on speed encourages glibness.

(3) The slow writer is thus at a double disadvantage. He is not able to put down as much as he would like or needs to; and he is unable to spare any time for preparatory thinking.

(4) The formality of the occasion is artificial and damaging. To work in silent serried ranks is unnatural; and unnatural work cannot by definition be either representative of the student or of true quality.

(5) To test a year's work – or maybe two or three years' – via a few three-hour papers is ludicrous. No student can do more than suggest the tip of an iceberg of learning and development in such a time.

(6) It is impossible to think carefully because of the need to write so fast. In addition, it is wrong to confuse clarity of thought with speed of answer, which exams inevitably do.

(7) Examiners have no contact with or knowledge of the students they judge. There is no room within such a set-up for personality or individuality: it is a cold business dependent on 'mark schemes' and 'right answers'. To fail someone is thus of no consequence to an examiner: he may even rather enjoy it.

(8) Passing exams is less a matter of true knowledge than an artful acquaintance with the tricks and quirks of 'the game'.

Even decisions like marriage involve
pressure

(9) There is no allowance for the fact that we all have our good days and our bad days. Inspiration should not be at the mercy of something as arbitrary as an exam-date.

(10) It is very difficult, if not impossible, to find out any *details* about one's performance. Worse, the procedure for challenging one's grade is so complicated and drawn out that it seems actively obstructive.

No doubt you could frame others; but I believe the above covers most of it.

There is enough truth in these objections for each one to be taken seriously; and as an amalgam it would seem to present a powerful case for the immediate abolition of such a cruel and unnatural practice.

The fact that exams are still very much with us suggests one of two things. Either all educational administrators *are* cruel or, worse, stupid; or the above objections are rather less convincing than they appear. With the latter notion in mind, here is a list of 'examination defences', or answers to the objections outlined above.

(1) Exams do put a premium on speed, yes. But why is this so awful?

A slow writer may have a mind as slow as a tortoise

All the jobs I can think of require you to think fast and efficiently at some time – and most of them require you to do so *often and as a matter of course*.

(2) It is a fallacy to equate speed with glibness. Every teacher – indeed, every person – has known hollow and obvious statements to be delivered with staggering ponderousness, often following an interminable 'incubation period'. Conversely, some of the greatest thinking in human history has visited the mind in question at tremendous speed. Not for nothing do we speak of marvellous ideas occurring to us 'in a flash'.

(3) The slow writer is somewhat disadvantaged, yes; and there are times when this is unjust. But *why* is the slow writer slow? Isn't it often because his *mind* works slowly too? I have known one or two excellent minds whose owners wrote slowly; but I've known far more tortoise-like writers whose minds were merely dogged and pedestrian.

Generally speaking, good minds work fast, and indifferent minds do not. Very often, a fast writer is fast because his mind is alert and in command of what he wants to say; the sad converse of the slow writer is evident all too often – he is sluggish and uncertain.*

* There are times, as I've stressed (see pages 71–73), when slow writing and thinking are valuable and necessary; but an exam is not one of them. A properly prepared and capable candidate *ought* to be able to think fast: if he cannot do so by this stage, it's doubtful if he knows his material.

(4) Exams are of course artificial – *up to a point*. They create pressure; and many people object to this as 'unnatural'. In fact, nothing could be less convincing. It is a truism that most of us do our best work under pressure; besides, most of our lives are conducted under pressure of some kind, as Isaiah Berlin's epigram wittily suggests. An exam *concentrates* this pressure, admittedly; but it does so in a controlled and flexible way, provided it has been wisely set. In addition . . .

(5) Examiners know perfectly well that a few three-hour papers cannot cover all that a student knows. Allowance for this fundamental point is not only made in the marking, but is built into every intelligently set paper (which means at least 95% of all papers set).

(6) The belief that an exam offers no time to think is an illusion fostered by panic-struck, unskilled examinees. There is *always* time to think: only the foolish or the manic try to write for every minute of the exam.

Furthermore, there is no reason at all why speed and clarity shouldn't go together. Clarity of thought is at least partly dependent on knowledge; and if you really know something it is instantly available to you. *Haste* will damage thought, certainly; but haste and speed are very different things, however similar on the surface. In the same way, *care* is of course important; but 'care' does not mean *merely* or even *chiefly* 'taking a long time'. It means fully concentrated, efficient effort; and that is more likely to attend a fast-working mind than a plodding one.

(7) Examiners are professional educators; they are experienced and well disposed towards the student. In any advanced exam, 'right answers' come into it much less than too many students still imagine. Far from penalizing individuality, examiners are looking to reward it. Furthermore, they dislike failing anyone, and great care and thought (by several examiners) is expended before any paper is confirmed as a fail.

(8) Those who think exam-passing is a kind of game of tricks and clever dodges are just plain stupid. If you are ever unlucky enough to get a teacher who plays in earnest the Russian Roulette of 'Let's guess the questions on this year's paper', take as little notice of him as you can. Only the ingenuous or the drearily cynical (which is the same thing, only worse) think of examiners as a bunch of academic bandits who must be 'outsmarted'.

However, there is, as we've stressed, a *skill* involved. We hope

Examination Russian Roulette: guessing
the questions on the exam paper

that we can set you on the way to acquiring it with the advice that
is to follow. The point is that you *won't* acquire it if you persist in
thinking of the matter as a rag-bag of tricks and corner-cutting
conning.

(9) 'Inspiration' has got little to do with knowledge, which is what
exams test. It has to do with primary creativity, such as painting,
composing, or poetry composition. It is possible that lack of
inspiration at the time could untypically affect say an Art student;
but usually you are given a two-week period in which to complete
your creative work (as opposed to your theoretical/critical
papers). If no 'inspiration' arrives during such a period, isn't it
equally likely that you're a bit low on actual *talent*?

In my experience, 'lack of inspiration' is, at least nine times out
of ten, an entirely bogus argument. It is nearly always an excuse
for either laziness or extreme ordinariness, or both; and it is a
complaint that should be regarded with deep suspicion.

(10) Finding out details about your grade, or challenging it, is, it is
true, a difficult business. But it can be done; and it often succeeds.
You usually have to pay for a re-mark; but it is done carefully and
thoroughly. Frequently, candidates never *do* challenge their
grade because they imagine it will be too much hassle, and a
waste of time to boot. Such a *post hoc, propter hoc* attitude really

won't do: if you feel strongly enough, and if it matters enough, *do it.*

In sum: provided they are sensibly set, and provided too that they are not the *only* mode of assessment,* exams are a valid and illuminating method of discovering a student's over-all ability. They test three central things which no other format yet devised can truly evaluate:

(a) They establish whether a student's knowledge is genuinely *his*. All other methods of assessment leave room for plagiarism, collaboration, or mere parrot-like regurgitation.
(b) Is this knowledge available at short notice, or indeed more or less instantly? Or does he need three days' preparation? I wouldn't be very happy hiring/working with the latter kind of mind. Would *you* trust someone that slow or uninformed?
(c) Can this knowledge be transformed into rapid and intelligible communication to others?

Nobody pretends exams are perfect. Injustices do occur; some students suffer from a genuine 'exam block'; and there are occasions when papers are poorly set. But such cases are rare; and while exams must continue to be carefully examined *themselves*, no-one has yet come up with a superior alternative – one that does what exams try to do and in a 'fairer' way. Until that occurs, you are it seems stuck with them. And, having listed their strengths and argued for their virtues (no doubt to your great annoyance!), let me now look at some matters of exam psychology more closely. To begin with, we'll take a detailed look at Examiners.

Examiners: friends or foes?

A couple of years ago, I carried out a word-association test with a class of fifteen-year-olds. There were twenty-two pupils (all girls) and I asked them to write down the first *two* words or phrases that came into their minds when I wrote the word 'Examiner' on the board. The breakdown of the forty-four selections was as follows:

Devious	*two*
Unreliable	*three*
Hostile	*four*

---

* At present, with certain exceptions, this is *not* true of 'A'-level courses in the UK, where the exams are the sole arbiter. I discuss this regrettable case later in the chapter: see page 162.

Sarcastic/Superior	*five*
Mercenary	*five*
Boring/Bored	*six*
Old	*seven*
Men	*twelve*

Not one of them mentioned a word that could remotely be taken as benevolent or encouraging. Without exception, the girls' associations were eloquent of fear, mistrust, dislike, and an overwhelming sense of 'them and us' (hence the high figure for 'men'!).

Most examiners are under 40

The anecdote has amusing aspects; but it is also sad. A student who tackles a paper with such an Identikit monster in mind as the recipient is hardly going to be at her best. And it is particularly sad because such a picture is almost awesomely *inaccurate*.

Here are a few cheering facts about examiners:

(1) Most exam-markers are under forty. At the time of writing I am thirty-six: I have been marking advanced exams for seven years, and at my last Examiners' Meeting I was one of the oldest present.

(2) Most markers do it for the money, yes; but that is never the *only* reason. Doing *anything* solely for cash is a dreadful, humiliating experience, and no-one does so voluntarily. Examiners take on this extra work because they are interested and sympathetic educators. You *need* to be interested in education as well as keen on money to

spend the first two weeks of a holiday marking scripts. *Truly* uninterested people wouldn't touch it.

(3)   The idea that examiners are hostile old hacks withering in jealousy is pure nonsense. Their job is much more agreeable if *you've* done a good job; so on that count alone they will be on your side. I have yet to meet an examiner who did not dislike failing a candidate. This is partly because it's depressing on a human level, and also because one has to be twice as careful, and spend twice as long, considering a 'borderline' script. A really good paper, on the other hand, is doubly pleasant: its quality makes it enjoyable to read, and its obvious class makes it easy (and therefore quick) to mark.

(4)   At least 40% of markers are women.

(5)   Examiners have all done exams themselves at some time, and so have a sympathetic awareness of what it's just been like for you. Moreover, they are quite clear about the limitations of the whole business, and as a result will approach your answers with a professional friendliness that probably allows you the benefit of the doubt eight times out of ten. The only candidates who are really 'hammered' are the arrogant, the plain silly, or the irredeemably ignorant and/or lazy; and in such cases one really has to say that it's the candidate's fault and not the exam's.

We can, in fact, sum up examiners and their job in these few short sentences:

Examiners are just people; so are you. They are hired to do one job: to find out if you can do what the exam asks you to do. If you do it well, you will score well. So forget all theories of 'them and us': in truth, it's them *and* you, working in harness to ensure, wherever possible, your success.

Remember, too, that you are not dependent on the whims of one examiner. The majority of scripts are read carefully by at least five people by the time the final grade/mark is determined. Extreme care is taken to ensure that the candidate gets a thorough and fair deal. Any unusual circumstances (illness, dyslexia, recent bereavement, etc.) are taken fully into account. All examining bodies canvass the school/college prior to the exam for an estimate of each candidate's likely performance and any major disparity between estimate and actual grade leads to all the papers being looked at again. Universities are no less thorough; and the Open University is, I have found, admirably caring and generous in its attitude to examinees. So, whatever terrors you still may have about exams in general, I hope I have eased your mind about the men and women who mark your scripts.

An approach to advanced exams: going beyond *mere* regurgitation

I have emphasized from the beginning that this book is designed for the voluntary student. One of the nice things about being a voluntary student is, obviously, that you're doing something you *want* to do; but this pleasing development has a rather more stringent corollary.

During your 'elementary' schooling, which in both America and England means roughly up to the age of sixteen, I'm sure you had to study a number of subjects which were less than riveting, and maybe one or two you were profoundly grateful to give up. But one of the built-in advantages of those days was the fact that a great deal of your work was *directly taught,* and, moreover, pre-digested for you. By this I mean that to succeed you *did not necessarily have to think creatively or independently.* Most of your work was a question of absorption and subsequent regurgitation. Of course, you had to *understand* the work fully in order for that regurgitation to be clear and accurate; but your work and progress were largely a question of how sound was your technical ability to digest and reproduce information and prepacked knowledge.

Now, I have no wish to sneer at such work and such qualities, or suggest that they are not important and admirable. Of course they are; but – and this is my point – you are about to find (if indeed you haven't already done so) that in terms of advanced study they are not enough on their own. True, they are the *basis* of everything; but unless you learn confidently to do some independent thinking of your own, your advanced study is going to remain somewhat humdrum.

You see, the inevitable characteristic of early learning (which includes all stages before the one you've now arrived at or returned to) is that it is *conservative.* While you are learning the basics, there is no need to do anything but trot out sensibly the factual or methodological knowledge you have been absorbing for years. But now, as an undergraduate or advanced student of whatever kind, your course requires you to do some real thinking, to have opinions, to 'wonder'. In short, you are now being implicitly asked to respond as a sophisticated individual, and to do rather more than behave like an efficient sponge.

Nowhere is this necessary change more vital than in examinations. Indeed, there is one concept that is such an insidious and damaging myth if allowed room in an advanced student's mind that it needs to be demolished right away. For although it is entirely laudable, and necessary, to 'want to get things right' when learning the elementary, basic techniques of a given subject, it is an aim which the advanced student should begin to treat with healthy scepticism.

Accuracy versus correctness: exams and 'the right answer'

Many advanced students make the forgivable but highly dangerous mistake of confusing the concepts 'accuracy' and 'correctness'.

Only a fool or a charlatan would deny the importance of accuracy. It is the basis of everything, and without it anything is just a shambles. If a recipe tells you to cook a dish in a moderate oven for thirty minutes, your guests aren't going to be over-delighted if you submit it to furnace-like temperatures for an hour and a quarter. In the same way, if a petrol-pump gauge promises you ten gallons, and you find out later that it was fixed/on the blink, so that all you actually received was ten *litres*, you aren't going to be terribly happy.

In the academic field, therefore, you can't expect to get away with, say, the proposition that 4×6 is 257, or even 25, any more than you can expect leniency in your submission that the Battle of Hastings took place in 1382, or that the French for 'man' is 'le bloke'.

Nevertheless, the point about all those examples is that they are *elementary* – in the sense of 'fundamental' rather than 'easy'. Yes, you need to obey oven temperatures and time, and you need to be able to trust the pump gauge. But it's a matter of taste/choice/*subtle debate* whether you add a little sour cream or some extra seasoning, or whether you select Texaco, BP, or Esso. The same is true for academic matters. You must ensure that your maths is accurate, and your spelling correct – you must, in short, get your *facts* right. But your use of those facts, your *interpretation* of them, is up to you, whether your subject is Physics, History, Economics, or anything else.

Of course, many students do realize this, as no doubt you do. At least, they realize it *in principle*. The fact remains that many such students fail to act on this theoretical awareness, and it *could* easily happen to you too. There are, it seems to me, two main reasons why this is so.

The first is the constraints of the exam itself. It isn't easy to relax in an exam (it *can* be done, however. See Appendix B), and because of this, one is often more cautious, more conservative than one normally is. The temptation is to 'play safe'; and this can easily mean shutting out most of the things that have made you a talented and successful student in the months before.

I'm very sympathetic to this syndrome; but it is important that you try not to 'tighten up' in such a way. I've stressed throughout that you will do better, and have more fun, if you stay yourself: this is *especially* true of the exam.

The second reason returns me to my point about the innate *conservatism* of your elementary schooling. In pre-advanced exams, there is not much difference between 'accuracy' and 'correctness'. The name of that earlier game is facts – it's about whether you 'know your stuff'. It would not be true to suggest that earlier work actively *prevents* you thinking in an independent, creative way; but the point is that there is no *need* for you to do so then. As a result, many able pupils deduce that there is apparently little value in trying to be 'different' or 'stimulating' in such a way. They gradually get the central message – that if they trot out their facts in a well-organized fashion, and do precisely what they're told, they pass. It's virtually as simple as that.

As I've said, this is entirely admirable, and harmless *provided that it is not thought to be a permanent law of* all *levels of study*. The trouble arises when students get into the long-term habit of equating 'accuracy' (the essential foundation) with 'correctness' or 'the right/only answer'. And I cannot emphasize too strongly that

in ADVANCED study, there is no such thing as ONE right answer.

In exams, many advanced students ignore this. Instead of answering questions in a natural way, they convince themselves that they must search for what the examiner thinks and wants them to say.

This is very bad policy for a number of reasons. For a start, it's self-evidently doomed, because you'll *never* know what an unknown examiner's opinions/tastes are! More subtly, and more importantly, you thus turn your back on the qualities that have made you a good student. Once you start thinking in terms of what you *ought* to say rather than what you feel/*want* to say, you're turning yourself into a studious zombie rather than a vigorous academic. Edgar's lines at the end of *King Lear* are a splendid model for any examinee:

The weight of this sad time we must obey,
Speak what we feel, not what we ought to say.

If you regard an exam as a 'sad time', you will find the 'weight'of the

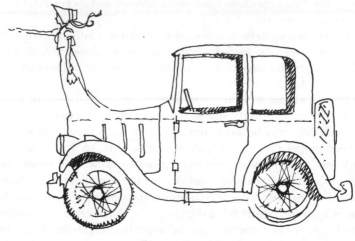

Jane Austin

occasion lessens considerably if you rid yourself of all *extra* constraints, especially that of searching for 'the right answer'. *If you apply your knowledge, and have a sound methodological and factual base, you will be fine.*

Naturally, all advanced study requires you to master a great deal of information/factual knowledge. I am not in the least suggesting that this level is unimportant. *Of course* you have to satisfy your assessors that you know what you're talking about; you *must* know your formulae/dates/vocabulary/laws/characters' names, and so on. As an English examiner, I encounter a rather alarming number of candidates who refer to Jane Austin, as if she's a literary sub-division of British Leyland; and many other howlers pepper any batch of scripts. Two particular favourites from papers I've marked are:

(1) 'In Hardy's novel, *Toss* of the *Derbyfields* . . .'
     and
(2) '*In Defoe's* great *play, Gulliver's Travels* . . .'

The second delighted me particularly: I think I wrote 'Close!' or 'one out of three isn't bad, I suppose' in the margin. But two serious points also arise from these examples. The first is that, clearly, they don't create the best possible impression (both howlers occurred in the essays' first paragraphs). But the second is that (so far as I remember) both candidates passed with some comfort. They may have made a ghastly error or two; but they also produced quite interesting, sound and responsive work.

In short: 'accuracy' is important, naturally. It means *getting the basics right*. But at any advanced level of study, that is *all* it means. The real quality of advanced work lies in its freshness, or its distinctness from other interpretations of the same material. Take a tip from something we've all had to study for at least several years – Maths, and specifically 'O'-level Maths. Anyone who has taken this subject will remember being told time and time again that one gets more credit for the 'working' than for the solution. The same is true for all advanced work. The credit (which, crudely, means *marks*) is earned by your method, your approach, *you*. Such things are far more vital than any notional sense you may have of 'correctness'. Don't ever forget that – especially in an exam.

Lastly in this section, before I go on to techniques useful in the exam room itself, let us look at some of the ways in which students approach exams, with a view to establishing how you can 'psych yourself up' sensibly (as opposed to damagingly!).

Do you sincerely want to do well in exams? Then *enjoy* them

I can clearly visualize some of you preparing to throw this book through the window, swearing loudly the while, as a result of the above sub-title. Please lower your arm, and bear with me for a moment!

I have argued throughout that successful study will be fun. This is as true for exams as all other aspects of your work – arguably *more* vital, since the pressure on you is greater. I believe it is essential for you to cultivate a *long-term attitude* that grows to regard the exam as a natural and exciting climax to a pleasurable course.

You may think such a remark silly. But it's a lot less silly than working yourself up into an induced panic, whereby the exam seems about as attractive as being on the wrong end of a thumb-screw. If you've worked well during the course, no exam should hold any terror for you. On the contrary, it ought to be a nice release, a chance to show everyone how good you are. For remember:

All good students are humble; but hardly any of them are modest.

I don't mean you should swank cockily into the exam room; still less do I advise you to assume smugly that it'll be 'a doddle'. But too much self-effacement is equally absurd. If you're properly humble, you know how much you *don't* know; but it's worth remembering that you're aware of that ignorance only because of all the things you *do* know.

Of all the annoying (and usually dishonest) attitudes I encounter as a teacher, the permanent prize always goes to the person whose demeanour and performance roughly add up to the proposition, 'I'm sure you won't be interested in what little me has to say.' Very often, such modesty (mysteriously held to be a virtue) is either a cover-up for simple laziness, or a coy invitation to be showered with boosting praise until such time as a beneficent, condescending contribution is offered in return.

So do not go modestly into that exam fight. Operate sanely on the premise that you know what you're doing and have enjoyed your work. The exam should then turn out to be a pleasant affair. After all, an exam is only different in its setting. The basic truths about your work and your pleasure in it remain unchanged.

I'm not so insensitive or stupid as to think that all exam fears can be cured by a few minutes' 'positive thinking'. Exams require a number of strengths and qualities (including sheer stamina) that do not material-ize very quickly. But if you can think of the exam in the terms I've outlined from an early stage in your work, it will be very fruitful. For the *opposite* approach, which we'll look at now, can be disastrous, and has no compensating factors whatever.

Negatively charged

Posturing excuses

How often have we heard a candidate aged ten, thirty, or fifty, just prior to entering the exam room, announce to all within earshot:

'I'm dreading this – I haven't done a stroke of work for weeks.'

It is an apparently simple, throwaway remark. But consider the number of powerful implicit messages that such a casual disclaimer sends out:

(1) It protects the speaker from failure, or at least the *humiliation* of failure. If he *does* fail, it will not be because he's inadequate, but because he didn't do 'a stroke of work'.

(2) Equally important, he's adding kudos to any possible *success*. If he passes, he will seem naturally gifted – someone who has no *need* to do 'a stroke of work'.

(3) The casual, what-the-hell tone establishes an immediate superior-ity over all those who are quietly wrecking their finger-nails, endowing him with an air of bravado and cool style.

(4) The impression created is one of lofty boredom. The underlying idea seems to be that only an idiot would *bother* to work for an exam.
(5) There is even the suggestion that he has had much better, more exciting things to do than *study*!

It almost seems a shame to pour cold water on such a blaze of virtuosity. But the fact is that all those implications are annihilated once it is realized that

> It is splendidly but utterly *untrue*. If he really *is* 'dreading' it, then he'll have been working all right, don't you worry. If on the other hand he *genuinely* hasn't done 'a stroke of work', then he's not dreading it at all – the whole exam ceased to have any meaning for him weeks ago. After all, 'dread' is not boring!

Tony Buzan wisely points out (*Use Your Head*, pp. 110–112) that such a syndrome can apply equally to the able student who knows he's made a 90% effort rather than a 100% one. Public disclaimers of this kind (so runs the psychology) protect you from the narrow failure to achieve a distinction just as winningly as from the dramatic failure to secure a pass. It is frightening how ingenious *all* of us can be when it comes to making excuses. If we expended just *half* that mental energy on doing the actual work, results would be amazing!

False pessimism and self-fulfilling prophecy
Unjustified, unearned confidence is not a happy quality; but there is *nothing* more devastating than false pessimism. At least the shock that awaits the false optimist can be salutary, showing him what has to be done in future. His self-esteem will be bruised, but it's unlikely to be obliterated at one go. The appalling thing about false pessimism is that it can destroy your real ability and its future potential long before they are tested. If you work yourself up into believing you're going to do badly, then I'm afraid the chances are that you *will*.

A sporting analogy usefully demonstrates this point. If you go into a rugby tackle *expecting* to be hurt, it is distinctly likely that you will be. Your body will be awkward and vulnerable, making injury much more probable. Similarly, if you are frightened of a hard ball (cricket or hockey) and imagine it will hurt if you try to catch it, then it probably will: your fingers will be stiff and angular, and your palms will be wincing well in advance of receiving the ball. Result: the ball will probably hit the fingers rather than the soft cushion of the palm, causing sharp pain at the least.

Exams are much the same. If you go into the room in a muck-sweat of panic, your brain ablaze with feverish anxiety, and your memory straining to remember everything you've ever been taught, you will be

(1) More or less exhausted by the time you read the paper.
(2) Already conditioned to think in terms of failure and the impossible difficulty of the whole exercise.

Jean-Paul Sartre once defined modesty as 'the virtue of the half-hearted'. Modesty's insidious cousin, false pessimism, takes *all* the heart out of you – and invariably for no reason. You can guard against it by cultivating an attitude that is far more cheerful . . .

'Si tu veux, tu peux'

The ideal mood in which to enter an exam room is keyed-up but expecting to perform at least adequately. The best analysis of this positive approach that I know of is by Adam Hall. It is from a thriller, but that does not detract from its astuteness:

'I subscribe to Coué, Maltz, and the Frenchman who said, "Si tu veux, tu peux." They all make the same point, but Coué put it quite well: in any contest between the imagination and the will, the imagination always wins.

An example would be: if the ship's been sunk under you and it's a ten-mile swim to the shore, you'll stand more chance of getting there by using imagination instead of will-power. You can grit your teeth and will yourself to do it, but the command is conscious, and your *subconscious* is on board for the trip and it can be a lead weight if left to its own little games: once it starts brooding about the black silent fifty-fathom void below your body, the will-power is going to lose a lot of steam. But if you bring in the subconscious to work *for* you, it means the imagination will be programmed in, and in place of a lead weight you've got yourself a propeller. Feed it the key image 'shore' and you're there already, prone as a log and coughing up water, but safe and alive.'*

The activity of exam-taking is rather less dramatic than Hall's example; but the principle is identical. 'Si tu veux, tu peux': if you want to, you can. Establish the right attitude – that is, a proper sense of confidence in your ability and preparedness – and the worst is over before you even sit down. You are ready for anything they can

* Hall, A. (1975) *The Striker Portfolio*, Fontana, London, p. 71.

reasonably throw at you, and you are positively looking forward to it. Such an approach won't guarantee success; but it will guarantee an absence of dry-up, panic, mental blocks, and that sudden sense of not being equal to anything you're asked.

Summary: exam-phobia – authentic or phoney?

Some students experience genuine, deep-rooted problems in exams. Their minds 'go blank', they get the shakes, their hands go numb, and they suffer from any number of sudden disabilities. Such cases need careful and caring help, and I hope I'd be the first to be sympathetic. But the vast majority of so-called 'exam-phobes' are not of this order. In my ten years as a teacher, I have come across only about half a dozen authentic cases. The rest are simply nervous, in a normal and healthy way. The trouble is, they don't *regard* it as normal and healthy. They aggravate their nerves by talking about it with their friends and colleagues, swopping horror-stories and exaggerations in a kind of masochistic game.

I use that last word advisedly. For I've noticed that a great number of students *enjoy* getting 'het up' about exams. Up to a point, this is both harmless and amusing, and is fine. But once it takes root it becomes a neurosis that can't be fully controlled. If you're such a student (and you'll know if you are), then try to act on some of the ideas and approaches I've outlined. They certainly won't do you any harm, and they may allow you to wrench yourself out of a pointless and damaging prejudice.

As I said at the beginning, exams are a perfectly rational, if imperfect, method of assessment. The major problem is that student unease about them is nearly always *irrational*. For a number of reasons and via a number of routes, student anguish about exams acquires a pathological dimension, ranging in intensity from anxiety to semi-hysteria. Such sudden lack of confidence and calm is, in the over-whelming majority of cases, quite unjustified. And it's as if the sufferers somehow *know* this – hence the way their irrational fears are quickly *rationalized* in the form of ostensibly intellectual objections to exams as 'cruel', 'unfair', and so on. But the process shouldn't be allowed to fool anybody – least of all, I hope, you yourself. Nearly all objections to exams are rooted in a gut response rather than a reasoned appraisal; and once you look clear-sightedly at what an exam sets out to do, and at your own abilities, I think you'll find that your gut returns to normal, de-shrunk and calm!

Postscript: the problem of 'A' Level (for UK students only)

Most advanced courses these days are only *partly* assessed through an exam. More and more the practice seems to be 50% exam, and 50% course-work through 'continuous assessment', or roughly those proportions. This seems to me to be eminently sensible, and humane. It preserves the unique and proper test that an exam affords, without allowing the inevitable limitations of such a method to govern all. It also gives the student a clearer sense of the over-all rhythm of his course, since he is regularly 'called to account' in his work and progress from an early stage.

Regrettably, this is not yet the case for nearly all 'A' Level courses. Some progress is being made in reducing the be-all, end-all nature of 'A' Level exams; but it's slow, and so far insubstantial. There is, I fear, little you can do for *yourself* in this matter: you're already at a stage, if you've embarked upon such a course, where the die is cast, since it would take years to effect a major change even if everybody started on it *now*. That is not to say you're at a worrying disadvantage: after all, it's the same for all your fellow 'A' Level colleagues/competitors. And it is because this book is designed for 'A' Level as well as tertiary students that Chris and I have devoted such a substantial amount of space to exams in general. But if, like us, you feel strongly that 'A' Level should not be so monolithic in its use of the final exam, then write to the Boards, to the LEAs, to the HMIs, as many of your teachers regularly do. For only, I think, when the administrators become fully and inescapably aware of a large body of opinion that holds such a method to be unwise, too narrow, and thus unfair and inefficient, will they seriously contemplate doing anything about it. That's how many University courses got changed; perhaps we can all help to do the same for 'A' Level.

14

● ● ● ● ●

Examinations: preparation hints

Chris Pope

I loathe examinations, as Richard Palmer has already told you. Thus this chapter, unlike those sandwiching it, is written by someone forced to accept that there is no alternative, and that exams are a necessary evil. This chapter is intended to give you ideas about how to prepare for exams. Beforehand, though, I would like to explain my dislike of them. I hope you appreciate my argument, because it doesn't condemn exams simply because they are disagreeable: it looks at them objectively, and might therefore help you to approach them rationally.

A further objection to exams

A perfect exam would seek out the candidates' true knowledge and understanding of a subject; a perfect examinee would perform exactly according to his potential; a perfect examiner would mark the papers without any subjective influence; and the results would accordingly reflect, accurately, the candidates' respective abilities in the subject.

But no exam, examinee or examiner is perfect. In the attempt to achieve perfection any exam system will become stereotyped – otherwise its standard would differ from year to year, and it would be obscure, thus becoming an initiative rather than a subject test. But a stereotyped system means discrimination against those who do not fit in. In other words, you can do badly despite having good knowledge of your subject, just because you did not respond to the exam as well as you should, or in the way the system required.

However unrepresentative the mark is, though, an important examination result is something with which you are stuck for life.

Worse, it is often used by society as the only measure of your academic abilities. This is why I object to exams, and why Part 3 of this book exists! But it's also why important exams are to be taken seriously, even if you profoundly disagree with them.

Examination techniques

Exam techniques could be defined as the art of proving to the examiners just how good you are and, where possible, using to your advantage any predictability that exists. It's largely a matter of tackling the exam clear-sightedly and sensibly, and slotting into the system as perfectly as possible without sacrificing any originality. The technique you adopt will depend entirely on you and the exam in question. It comes largely with experience and good judgement.

Since this is a general study aid and no two exams are the same, all Richard and I can do is to suggest ways in which you might improve yourself. It's up to you to determine your exact method of preparation, and thus your technique. If you are still in difficulty after reading this section of the book, your teachers should be able to help – there are more specific aids on the market too.

Revision timing

If you have followed the advice in the book so far, by the time the exams approach you will have understood everything and it will all be stuck firmly in your long-term memory. There will therefore be no need to do any revision at all, and you'll be ready to take the advice given by a certain study aid I once read – leave your books behind and spend a fortnight before the exam on a tropical island, relaxing and sampling the local delights. Personally, my nerves would oblige me to spend the fortnight so intoxicated that the other local delights would have to remain unsampled – and that's taking no account of the exam performance afterwards! But everyone is different. If you find such holidays the key to exam success, don't let me spoil your enjoyment!

But let's face it, for most of us revision will occupy us right up to the exams, and it will involve going over material that we forgot long ago. It's also alarming finding out how much you *have* forgotten! This is why it's crucial to ascertain *very early on* (i.e. months rather than weeks before) how much work there is to be done, and that will mean flicking through all your notes and probably doing a past paper too. It's also important, where applicable, to get hold of a copy of the exam syllabus.

This should put your notes into perspective, and show you where the loopholes in your notes and knowledge are.

Once you know how much work there is to be done, it's up to you to decide *when* to start revising. I have always found a timetable necessary to give me an idea of how close the exams are – I can never truly accept that they are approaching until it's too late! Whatever your strategy, always leave yourself what seems to be far too much time. It's bound to be too little! I also strongly advise you to leave a lot of time for doing past papers, because (for the reasons I am about to set out) going through these is often just as important as revision of a theoretical nature.

Past papers

Arguably the most direct way of improving exam technique is to go through as many previous years' papers as possible. With subjects such as literature, where the set books change from year to year, it is usually easy to make up your own questions to be answered in exam conditions. As I've already stressed, you will have to leave plenty of time between finishing 'primary' revision and the exam for this. (If you haven't left enough time for revision itself, looking through past papers should show you where it is best to take short-cuts.) Clearly, the papers will show up any remaining gaps in your knowledge – often where you don't expect them! But this is valuable in two ways: one, it identifies the gaps precisely, thus enabling you to 'plug' them efficiently through further revision; and two, it will increase your experience and methodological prowess, and thus bolster your self-confidence. The practice clarifies, in short, both knowledge and technique.

In order to improve you must look at each answer, perhaps a couple of days later, from the examiner's point of view. It's worth listing the kind of things to be on the look-out for:

(1) How many good points have you made?
(2) How many more could you have inserted?
(3) Have you actually answered the question?
(4) Are there any irrelevant parts you could have omitted?
(5) Could the answer have been clearer?
(6) How easy is a stranger going to find your handwriting?

Be honest about these, and never give yourself the benefit of the doubt.

A major benefit of such practice is that it will make you conscious of all those questions when writing the answer itself, on the day. With subjects such as literature, where there is no right or wrong as such, you will have to ask your teacher to look over your answers as well, and tell you if there's a weakness in your argument, or suggest any further improvements that could be made in addition to the ones you've listed yourself. At first you may be startled by how badly you do – I always am! But you will gradually get better.

As well as simply answering questions, you should also look at all the papers together to determine your rough strategy during the exam. You must know how many marks each section/question carries and the time allowed for each. This allows you to establish roughly in what order to tackle the questions and also to determine where to take short-cuts should you run short of time (depending, for instance, on whether you'll get more credit for answering three questions completely or four incompletely). With some subjects there are topics which come up regularly. Without wanting to encourage you to 'guess the questions on this year's paper' (a dangerous practice which Richard has quite correctly condemned), I suggest you would be silly to ignore recurring topics.

By the time you take the exam, the format and requisite thought processes will be familiar, you will know the standard expected, and you will be used to answering in the time allowed. You might even get a question similar to one you've answered before! All this gives you little to be apprehensive about, and you should therefore possess the vital streak of controlled confidence necessary to do as well as possible.

The day of the exam

By this time you should be in no doubt about any of the factors mentioned above, including time-allowance and marks for each question. You must also have had a good sleep the night before.

If the exam is in the morning, your pens, pencils, etc., should have been prepared the evening before so as to avoid a last-minute panic. Get up early enough to leave yourself plenty of time. However, there is no point in sacrificing sleep for an early-morning revision session as the freshness and energy you lose will not be compensated for by the small amount of knowledge you might gain.

If the exam is in the afternoon, I have always found a gentle look over a past question or two a good way of 'ticking over' in the morning without losing too much energy. If there are some quotes or formulae that you have always found hard to memorize, it's worth trying to get them into your short-term memory. But launching into full-scale revision is, for the reasons I gave above, stupid. You should assemble your pens, ink, pencils, sharpener, ruler, compass, calculators (with new/recharged batteries), tables and all other necessary bits and pieces well before it's time to go. Then you will have half an hour or so to lie down, listen to some music, and generally force yourself to relax before leaving.

Allow a lot of time for any journey that has to be made – don't let a cancelled train or late bus take you by surprise! But only arrive at the exam hall itself about ten minutes before the exam is due to start. Any earlier, and you'll have an empty time in which to panic; any later, and you'll be rushed and won't have time to compose yourself.

The first thing to do when you sit down at your desk is to make yourself comfortable and arrange your paraphernalia for quick access later. At this point I usually put my name at the top of as many sheets of paper as possible. This allows the hand to 'warm up' – and it also enables a quick escape at the end!

Richard deals with what to do in the exam itself in considerable detail in the next chapter; so all I will do before handing over to him is to list a few obvious points of technique that I have found particularly useful:

(1) Answer the easier questions first. This boosts morale, and should leave you with extra time to deal with the harder questions later.

(2) If the questions are 'structured' (i.e. in several parts, with fixed mark allocations for each part), answer each part clearly and concisely, with a new paragraph for each point you make. The length of your answer will obviously depend on the number of marks being given: make at least as many points as there are marks to be obtained.

(3) Remember that you're taking a gamble answering a question on a topic you have not prepared, and that gambles either come off very well or – more often in my experience – very badly indeed.

(4) In multiple-choice papers, don't change your first answer, however tempting it may be, unless you're *positive* that the second decision is correct. The second answer is usually wrong!

(5) *Never panic!*

15
● ● ● ● ●

Examinations: skills and techniques

We have nothing to fear but fear itself.
F. D. Roosevelt

Throughout the previous two chapters in this section, we have assumed three things.

(1) That you've done a reasonable amount of work.
(2) That there's a fair chance of you passing. Many talented students find certain subjects inimical to them at times: to cite a personal example, I could never cope with Physics, from a very early stage. I had no real idea what I was doing, and came to the exam regarding my candidacy as an unfunny but inescapable joke. I recorded a majestic 9%! No 'exam technique' could have helped: I was far too ignorant.
(3) That you *want* to pass. Such a remark may seem just silly; but there *are* people who like attending exams simply because it gives them something to do and talk about. They have no interest in the work itself, and thus no interest in succeeding. There aren't many such types, but they do exist: they are the least impressive examples of 'the eternal student'.

Assuming that all three apply, let's move on to specific skills and methods that will help you to perform at your absolute best on the day itself.

Revision

I have little to add to what I said in Chapter 5 (see pages 55–56), and to Chris's admirable advice in the last chapter. I'd just like to reiterate four basic guidelines:

(1) Memory relies partially on environment. If possible, therefore, visit and inspect the place where you'll be sitting the exam. This will reduce the disagreeable awe you feel when entering the place on the day; and the consequent familiarity will enable you to relax and think more efficiently. If you can arrange to do some of your revision in the exam centre as well, so much the better.

(2) When revising, look *critically* at your work. Chris has shown you how to do this with practice answers; but you should do it with the body of your course-work as well. Correlate your teachers' marginal comments with your own sense of how good you *now* feel the work to be, and make notes accordingly. Log your discoveries and plug the gaps you've become aware of. This, as Chris stresses, increases both your knowledge and your confident awareness of how far you've developed.

(3) *Don't try to revise too much, or work all the time.* Your stamina is about to be tested, as well as your knowledge. You need to be fit and relaxed to succeed at exams. So you must turn off and 'get away from it all', regularly and without shame or worry.

(4) Try to regard your revision period as a 'working holiday'. *Enjoy* the respite from regular classes: work intensively and seriously, yes – but have some fun too It'll make you feel good – and it's worth pointing out that few triumphant students are either pasty or miserable!

The exam itself

Before and after writing

A lot of students wreck their chances of exam-success before they even pick up their pens to start their first answer. So before that moment arrives, make sure that you've accomplished/understood the following five things.

1. Compose yourself

Get to the exam hall about ten minutes before the exam is due to begin. Try to relax as much as you can: those meaningless fat-chewing conversations are a *good* idea, however inane – if only because they ease your mind by revealing that others are just as nervous as you! If you prefer to be alone and silent, then take a crossword puzzle or something similar to fill those few minutes: it will 'warm up' your brain without allowing you to focus grimly on the approaching 'crunch', which can induce panic.

2. Nerves

For a start, don't *worry* about being nervous. It is a healthy and good sign. You are about to *perform*; and any performer – actor, footballer, musician, politician, TV weatherman – *should* be nervous just before starting. Indeed, experienced performers are only worried when they are *not* nervous: it suggests they are too 'laid back', or simply uninterested. A sharp, heightened sense of being alive is admirable – what we call being 'keyed up'. Adrenalin will charge you up perfectly and naturally, and ensure that you are at your most alert. No-one else can do it for you, and you certainly can't get it out of a bottle of *any* shape!

3. The first few minutes

Once at your desk, you'll have a few minutes while the papers are laid out, people settle, and so on. *Use* this time: get properly comfortable; look around you and banish that inevitable sense of strangeness; set out your pens, etc., for easy access; jot down any notes/reminders you feel like making; and try to relax – deep breaths and muscle tensing-and-relaxing exercise may help. (See Appendix C.)

4. The exam paper

When you get your paper and/or instructions to open it, *take it easy for at least two minutes*. Read it; and then read it again. Don't try to frame answers right away; just let the questions sink into you naturally: the brain will register most of the essential information without you having to push it in any way. Yes, you're under time-pressure; but a 100 m.p.h. charge at it from the absolute outset makes no sense at all. 'Festina lente' is another wise Roman tag:* your speed will be much the more efficient for having settled into a relaxed groove first.

5. Understanding the questions

Be quite sure you've fully ingested all the instructions – including the questions' precise wording. Any old fool can *read* a question; what you've got to do is *understand* its exact requirements. These days, all exam papers 'advertise' such important matters by the use of heavy type – word limits, numbers of examples to be included, methodological instructions, etc.; but it is still a good idea to highlight them

---

* Literally, 'hurry slowly'. An English equivalent might be 'more haste, less speed'.

further by encircling them in red biro, or whatever method you find works best.

This is especially advisable in that not *all* crucial instructions *are* in heavy type. Take particular note of all instructive verbs, and make sure you're absolutely clear on what each one involves. For example, the verbs 'describe' and 'explain' may seem virtually synonymous at first sight; but they are not. Consider the difference between these two questions:

(1) Describe the rise of Hitler.
(2) Explain the rise of Hitler.

I am not a historian; but even to an amateur like myself, it is clear that the first question asks for an 'objective' historiographical account, listing stages, events, and what we will call 'facts'. The second question, on the other hand, is much more a matter of interpretation, involving a consideration of mass psychology, of the emotional appeal of Fascism, and an understanding of the way mania can take hold of a nation. Question 1, in short, demands an account that is essentially *'public'* or *external*, while Question 2 requires a more *intuitive* or *internal*, *psychological* approach. They are, in fact, sufficiently different for there to be no reason why the two answers should more than vaguely overlap in terms of their basic material.

So be sure you've sorted such subtleties out before you begin. Your teacher will have (or certainly *should* have) covered such vital distinctions during the course; and it's especially important to remember them *now*.

There is one other vital thing to bear in mind before starting, even though it doesn't come into play until *after* you've written the answers. It is this:

Always try to leave yourself ten minutes to read through your answers at the end.

To have a good chance of achieving this, you must 'programme' it into your planning *at the beginning*. You might even set the alarm on your watch (if you have such a thing) to remind you forcibly.

I *know* every teacher advises you to do this, and that it's a predictable and boring remark. But I also know that at least 90% of students fail to act on it – not out of defiance or contempt, but because they simply don't remember until it's too late. But its benefits can be considerable:

(1) If you check ruthlessly for errors, flab, lack of clarity in both expression and handwriting, you will forestall quite a number of

the *examiner's* discoveries, and thus improve your chances quite considerably.

(2) It is in any event a much more efficient use of that time than the frantic addition of a further paragraph or two to your final answer. Remember that by that stage the examiner's judgement will be more-or-less formed. Last-minute thoughts are unlikely to affect it very much, if at all; but tightening and polishing *earlier* answers might well do so.

(3) Because your mind will be that little bit more relaxed, it's highly possible that a snappy phrase/the right word/any kind of 'missing link' will now occur to you where previously you had not time or inclination to 'let it come'.

(4) You will almost certainly feel better when 'Time' is called; and if you're doing another paper that day, such well-being is an important bonus.

Writing your answers

So far, our advice ought to be familiar to you: you'll have heard most of it before from your teachers. Don't let such familiarity breed contempt: remember that more people fail exams (or do less well than they should) by carelessly ignoring such advice than through lack of ability. Now, however, I'd like to offer some tips and advice that you may not have encountered.

Let's assume that everything is 'set up' soundly and well. That is to say, you have:

(1) Been adequately taught.
(2) Worked hard.
(3) Settled yourself in the exam room in a relaxed and alert way.
(4) Taken full note of all the rubric and all the requirements of the paper.
(5) Succeeded in banishing panic, and now feel quietly confident.

How can you ensure that you 'perform' at your best?

The first thing to do, regardless of subject, is

Get some ideas down on paper as soon as you can.

On the whole, I *don't* advise you to begin writing the actual answer straightaway. There can be exceptions: if, for example, you spot a question that you *know* you can do well, then go ahead – it will boost morale by getting you off to a flying start. But it's more likely that you'll need more of a 'warm up' before taking off. So use an 'energizing pattern' such as I describe in Chapter 8. This will take only a few moments, will 'ignite' your mind fully, and (best of all) give you a wealth of visual triggers to aid your progression from point to point and from argument to argument.

Next, map out an introductory paragraph in your mind – *and then abandon it.* Unless you have a particular facility in constructing short, pithy introductions (it's an unusual quality, and you'll have been told if you possess it), it is always best – *especially in an exam* – to get right into the substance of your argument. I would say that 70% of the exam-paper introductions that I read (at all levels) are a waste of time – pleasantly written but vacuous. And I can reinforce this argument by letting you into a 'secret' that invariably surprises most of the students I talk to. I can best introduce it with the question

Roughly how long do you think an examiner will spend reading and marking your script?

I've had answers ranging from 'twenty minutes' to 'over an hour'. In fact, an experienced marker will aim to do an average of five to six scripts an hour – which means that you have *approximately ten minutes of his time* to make your quality count.

This isn't meant to frighten but to help you; and perhaps a brief look at the inside facts of an examiner's task will clarify my argument and further ease your mind.

The examiner's timetable: an example

I mark 'A'-level papers in the summer, and Open University papers in early November. The schedule and workload is remarkably similar:

(1) I receive, on average, between 100 and 140 scripts.
(2) Each script comprises three or four essays, with an over-all length of about 10–12 sides of A4 paper.
(3) My 'deadline' for the return of scripts and the submission of mark-sheets and reports is about a fortnight from the day they reach me.
(4) Like the vast majority of examiners, I am usually working at my full-time job as well during the marking period.

You don't need a calculator to work out what this means. Your script will be part of a batch that the examiner has to work through at an over-all rate of *ten per day*. He will have the week-end to 'catch up', in case one or two week-days have found him too busy to fulfil his daily quota; but the point is that he simply hasn't got the *time* to dwell on your essays and answers in the fashion that your teachers have done over the months.

You must *not* think that, as a result, his assessment of your work will be slapdash and superficial, or that you're solely at the mercy of one such tearaway! For the perhaps-alarming schedule I've outlined has the following, more comforting, corollaries:

(1) Examiners are experienced professionals who have acquired the ability to assess work fairly and incisively in such short periods. A *new* examiner will take longer, as I did: the speed comes with practice, like most things.

(2) The reason our deadlines are so 'squashed' is that, once the scripts are returned to HQ, the Chief Examiners/Awarders spend over a *month* carefully correlating marks, patterns of distribution, and so on. *Our* task is made fast so that *their* job – deciding your grade over *all* the papers – can be done with proper care and unpressured judiciousness.

(3) This means that your script will, in all likelihood, be read by *several* examiners by the time your grade is determined.

So don't be alarmed – your performance will not be judged solely on that first ten-minute assessment. But it does mean that you should bear in mind the golden rule

When writing your answer, don't hang about – get into it right away.

Grab your examiner's attention; make him sit up and say, 'This one knows what he's doing'. It's always a pleasure to mark scripts that have a sense of purpose and vigorous clarity; and such qualities nearly always render your *material* cogent and enjoyable.

'Stating one's terms'

There is one kind of an essay, even so, where an introduction is essential. It's the one where you *have to define* what is to be the basis or 'angle' of your answer. An example will soon establish what I mean.

A recent English Literature paper included this question on Milton:

'Examine the ways in which Milton's style assists the argument in *Paradise Lost, Book IV.*'

The incautious student would say to himself: 'Nice one! It's the banker-question on Milton's use of language – plus the Biblical story, of course. I *like* it!' Well, partly, yes; but crucially, *no*. It's not a 'trick' question; but it's more subtle than such a breezy reaction recognizes.

The point is, you cannot possibly answer this question properly until you've defined *what* Milton's argument *is*. Your answer requires a brief introduction, summarizing that argument: *then*, and only then, can you go on to show how his use of *Genesis* and the English language reveals and endorses that argument.

You might say that this is obvious enough; but it was sobering – and sad – how many (quite able) students failed to do it. As a result a good deal of their stylistic analysis – while good enough for a *pass* – was insufficiently locked-on to the question's real focus to impress. And, by the way, it doesn't really matter if your subject is Physics or Economics rather than English Literature: the principle I'm outlining should be evident, and applies to all disciplines:

If you need to 'state your terms', do so, clearly and quickly. Otherwise, just get on with it. Don't offer 'appetizers': hit the 'main course' more or less at once.

When in doubt, be interesting: show them you can think

I've discussed this several times already: all I want to do here is to stress the importance of being fresh and individual in this your final test.

You *must* do what the question tells you to do, naturally. Being 'interesting' does *not* mean 'bending' the question to your own focus regardless of its specific requirements. But you nevertheless have room within those requirements to produce your own answer, as opposed to the kind of dull, worthy but predictable version that is devoid of personality. This is especially true if (as I'd hope) you're after a really good result rather than just a pass:

Merely trotting-out pre-digested stuff is not enough to secure a superior grade. You must show that you can respond as an individual mind. In short, you must show that you can *think*.

Most exams, at all levels, are devised with a Lowest Common Denominator in mind. That is, the 'pass' level is neither scary nor very prestigious. If the five things that I list on page 172 apply to you, there's very little chance of you failing. But if you're interested in doing a bit more than just *passing*, you need to make *yourself* felt. So:

(1) Don't be too 'holy'. If you've got something negative to say, and

you *feel* it genuinely, then go ahead and say it. If you *pretend* to be impressed with something when you're not, it will show – badly.

(2) Never apologize. By this I partly mean that you should avoid the kind of phrase I'm about to analyse in Appendix A on style – the time-wasting and curiously undermining emptiness of 'apologies' such as 'in my opinion', 'I think', 'I would say that . . .', and so on. But I also mean that you should both trust your responses and present them straightforwardly. Very few people really object to what a cogent and honest mind has to say in any circumstances; and that is perhaps truest of all in an exam.

(3) Never 'rave' emptily. Such remarks as:

> *'Shakespeare's brilliant play is quite wonderful'*
>   or
> *'Turner is a fantastic painter who really turns me on'*

are not only useless but faintly disagreeable. I've encountered both those statements in exam papers I've marked, and they strike me as mere crawling waffle!

Turner turns one on

(4) Equally, avoid *arrogant* criticism – that is, snooty but *unsupported* judgements. An exaggerated example might be:

> *'Chaucer's middlebrow wisdom about unimportant and extinct matters renders him merely dull. Besides, he can't spell.'*

(5) In short: whatever you do – praise or criticism – say what you feel, but say it in a fashion that is measured and, for want of a better word, 'polite'. Always try to imagine that you're having some kind of a *dialogue* with your examiner – a meeting of two interested and interesting minds.

Conclusion: don't be frightened

I've headlined this chapter with a wise remark by one of the greatest Presidents of the United States. His words are by now a cliché; but they still have value for anyone who cultivates either excessive modesty or self-induced nervousness – about anything, but particularly about exams. Although I've warned you about arrogance, the fact is that very few students ever make *that* error: far more – indeed, *far too many* – students reduce their impact through coyness or needless diffidence.

Above all, stop yourself using fear as an *excuse*. It is always tempting to do this – it gives you a first-class and apparently unanswerable get-out. But remember: people may be sorry for you if you say, 'I messed up the exam – I was too scared to do myself justice'. They may even *believe* you. But they won't *admire* you – how can they? You've had your chance; and you've blown it. As I've said, on a few occasions, such an event will be a *genuine* injustice; but far more often, it'll be nobody's fault but the candidate's.

I'm not trying to preach. If you've followed some of the advice in this book, you'll be aware of how able you can be, and that exam success is comfortably – and *enjoyably* – within your grasp. I'll end with this revelation, although he won't thank me for it: Chris Pope – who loathes exams – has this track record at the time of writing:

'O' Levels: 12   Number of Grade 'A's: 12
'A' Levels: 4 (Double Maths; Physics; Music)   Grade 'A's: 4

Not bad, eh?! But I asked Chris to collaborate on this book not because of those magnificent results, but because of his approach, his no-nonsense sensibleness, and his *enjoyment* of his work. I am convinced that it is those qualities as much as his actual ability that occasioned that unimprovable performance. *You* can do it too. Good luck to you; but, if you've studied well (and I hope this book has helped you to do so), then you don't need *luck*: all you have to do is just *do it*.

APPENDIX A

● ● ● ● ●

Some notes on style

When one finds a natural style, one is amazed and delighted;
for where one expected to see an author, one discovers a man.

Blaise Pascal

Throughout this book, I've urged you to stay yourself as far as possible, in all things. And as Pascal suggests above, it will be a notable strength if you can extend this principle to the way you write.

Why one person should write well where another (of equal intelligence) writes badly is often exceptionally difficult to say; and I could not hope to cover all or even most of the reasons in these few pages. What I do want to do is suggest *one* reason, examine it briefly, and then move on to some specific tips or guidelines that will help you to write well – or at least prevent you from certain common kinds of *bad* writing.

A good style takes many years to acquire. And I'm becoming more and more convinced that one reason why is that it takes many of us several years to *unlearn* the dreadful stylistic habits we begin to form at the onset of adolescence – at the time, that is, when we lose (sometimes for ever) the natural unselfconsciousness of childhood.

Small children are of course limited writers; but their style is invariably appealing, often very funny, and usually clear and sharp. That judgement owes nothing to sentimentality. Children write in such a fresh way because language, like most other experience, is still fresh for *them*. They may not know many words; because of this, the words they *do* know have a huge charm – almost a touch of magic – and the pleasure they get in using them results in a direct and natural expression that is itself a pleasure to experience.

Once we get used to language, its charm can fade; and this decline often coincides with the time (adolescence) when we suddenly start to feel awkward and hesitant, when we are acutely aware of others' awareness of us, and determined above all things not to look foolish. It is at this stage that we start to develop 'protective layers' of personality, or what the German psychologist Wilhelm Reich beautifully defined as 'character armour'. And one of the most formidable pieces of this armour is our language and how we deploy it. Whereas the child is quite unthinking and natural in giving tongue, the adolescent is cautious, wary, and very self-conscious. Often silence is preferred; otherwise, something non-committal, deliberately vague, or positively obstructive. It is as adolescents that we first learn to use language to *disguise* or *hide* our meaning rather than express it. And it is then too that we start to come under the influence of *public* modes of language. We become aware, however vaguely, of the ways in which politicians and other public figures express themselves; we recognize more and more the properties of 'formal' speech and writing; we become accustomed, in short, to adult language. And the point I want to emphasize is that

A great deal of 'adult' or 'formal' language is ugly, dull and obscure.

Of course, at any given time there are countless exceptions to this: I am not as arrogant or as élitist as that remark might imply. But next time you watch TV news, or listen to a current affairs programme, make a point of noting the language that is used. I bet that you will hear several of these expressions:

  (1) 'In this day and age'
  (2) 'At this moment in time'
  (3) 'Whys and wherefores'
  (4) 'Obtaining maximum potential advantage'
  (5) 'My members' material aspirations have been betrayed'
  (6) 'Industrial action'
  (7) 'We have made it absolutely clear that . . .'
  (8) 'It is a well-known fact that . . .'
  (9) 'The site has been rationalized'
(10) 'Strike potential'

I have heard all ten used during TV news over the last few months. They share a common ghastliness that I discuss in a moment; but they also fall into four distinct groups, each of which exhibits a separate vice.

    (1), (2) and (3) are simply illiterate. They either indulge a needless repetition ('why' *means* 'wherefore') or, as in (2)'s case, solemnly imply a ludicrous distinction (as if it were somehow possible to have 'a moment' that *wasn't* 'in time' – in *space*, perhaps?).

    (4) and (5) are pompous, ugly inflations of simple phrases. (4) means

'doing one's best', while (5) is a rotund (and therefore dishonest) way of saying 'my members haven't been given the money they wanted'.

(6), (7) and (8) mean the exact *opposite* of what they claim to say. (6) means 'on strike'; (7) is the invariable preamble to the revelation of a policy or opinion that is news to everyone; and (8) almost always prefaces something that is neither well known nor a fact.

(9) and (10) are cynical euphemisms. (9) was used as a curious way of informing us that a number of buildings had been demolished; while (10), of course, is a standard phrase of Nuke-speak – the language of nuclear weaponry: it means the ability to kill x millions of people within a few minutes.

I said they share one ghastly feature: it is that they are all clichés. They are all irreducibly *boring* – stale, plodding, and so predictable that, once the first word is articulated, the rest follow as if hyphenated, or part of a magnetized sequence. They are empty formulae, used either by people who have no relation to what they're saying, or else who want to disguise and distort its true nature.

Our language, regrettably, teems with expressions like those. And the insidious thing about them is their apparent respectability, and the belief – connived at by people who ought to know better – that there's something weighty and impressive about them. Many people who use that loathsome expression, 'on-going situation', don't do so because they have no feeling for language, or because they really think it's a crisp and useful phrase: they do it because they imagine it's the right thing to do, having heard distinguished (or at least public) figures use it.

This is even more likely to be a problem for those of you who are *already* adults. Because you hear your peers, many of them distinguished, using certain phrases and styles of speech, you may feel that they offer admirable contemporary models. While the eighteen-year-old apes such linguistic behaviour under the impression that it will make him seem *more* adult, the older student does so because he is wary of departing from what he hears and sees to be established practice.

I believe this is why so many students have so much trouble forging a clear and efficient style. Their sense of *what* they want to say is, far more often than not in my experience, good; but they are confused about *how* they should say it. Faced with the apparent model provided by adults in the public eye (and quite a lot of adults who aren't), they set about acquiring the 'correct' approach, the 'right' phrases, the 'impressive' expressions that will guarantee them suitable stylistic maturity and *gravitas*. This is both sad and damaging. The desire to be orthodox, or just acceptably articulate, leads to a denial of natural instincts, replaced by a stuffy and above all wasteful stodge.

You see, a lot of adults, particularly those in public life, spend a lot of time deliberately saying nothing in a good many words. You can prove this to yourself next time you watch the news. Make a note of how many times a reporter takes one minute of fast talking to say virtually nothing. Listen to the number of politicians or diplomats who trot out fluent sentences that mean absolutely nothing, or else suggest the opposite of what the words seem to say. I'm not saying the news is either valueless or illiterate; but it is both instructive and richly comic to discover how much pure *waffle* it contains.

As a student, you must be on your guard against aping the examples that surround you. Go for the simple phrase always; when in doubt choose the most direct word possible; and above all try to

Listen **to what you write**

I don't mean you need to *recite* it (although this isn't a bad idea), but that you should try to hear with your 'inner ear' what you're writing. A couple of excellent, simple guidelines are worth bearing in mind:

If it *feels* good, it very probably *is* good: keep it.
      and conversely
If it *sounds* odd, it very probably *is* odd – and unclear as well: change it.

Perhaps most of all, *don't waffle.* Politicians waffle because they're 'on the spot': they need either to disguise the fact that they don't altogether know what they're talking about, or to prevent the interviewer penetrating their *real* motives, activities, and achievements. Up to a point, that's fair enough: it's part of the 'game' they involve themselves in with the media (who are often equally vacuous). But it's no part of a student's 'game' to be vague, distortive or just plain empty. Be sure that

When you've nothing to say, don't say it. And if you *have* got something to say, do so in as unadorned and direct a way as you can.

There are certain limits, of course. I don't advise you to start peppering your essays with obscenities or street-slang – that's a bit *too* direct! In fact, as you've no doubt been advised, slang of most kinds is probably best avoided. However, I'm sure I'm not alone in thinking that a few 'slips' into refreshing slang are much to be preferred to the kind of turgid, more 'respectable' level of expression that I discuss above.

New students, whatever their actual age, are bound to feel a touch adolescent. This is natural and in many respects nice: it brings a youthfulness back to you, and with it the kind of energy and enquiring interest that are commonly associated with being young. But all adolescents, whether actual or 'symbolic', feel a great need for some kind of uniformity, or indeed a uniform: what seems to be 'rebellion' or 'rejection' in teenagers, for example, is very often only a desire to find a *different* uniform from others, one that is distinct from their parents but gives them unity elsewhere. (This explains, for instance, why ostensibly rebellious movements like Punk, New Romantics, and all the rest acquire a recognizable 'uniform' which itself becomes a 'fashion' mobilized by market forces.) Don't, however, let this natural inclination extend to your writing. Hold on to all that is most you in your style, all that is most natural and most deeply formed. To help you do this, there now follow some short sections on phrases to avoid and useful approaches to adopt.

1. Dead expressions I: padding

It's a good rule of thumb not to 'apologize' for what you're about to say or 'wind yourself up' into it, but just to say it. So avoid the kind of expressions that follow below, noting why they are so unhelpful:

It is interesting to note that . . .	This remark kills all interest at once.
It may perhaps be said that . . .	Well, why shouldn't it be?
It is worthy of note that . . .	Pompous; and it often prefaces obvious remarks.
We can safely say that . . .	If it's *that* safe, why not just say it?
From certain points of view . . .	*Whose* point of view? Looks merely vague and timid.

Most such remarks are useless. They create an impression both flabby and over-cautious, and they fall dully on the eye. Reserve them for those times when there really *is* a doubt, when you truly *are* advancing an idea that is unusual or controversial, or when something out of the common run is at issue. Otherwise, just trust yourself: if your knowledge and thinking are sound, you don't need to 'stutter' in this way.

Similarly, avoid such compounds as:

The poet succeeds in creating an arresting picture . . .
Dickens manages to convince us . . .
Shakespeare is trying to put over the point that . . .

In the first place they are clumsy; in the second place they are flabby (the slim-line 'creates', 'convinces' and 'puts over' will do just as well, and do it more tautly); and in the third place they are all faintly disagreeable:

'Succeeds in creating . . .'	suggests that the poor old poet had a hell of a time getting his work up to standard.
'Manages to convince . . .'	is rather patronizing, as if one's giving him a Good Mark ('Well done, Dickens, old chap').
'Shakespeare is trying to . . .'	is nearly always inaccurate, and in an unfortunate way. It's not Shakespeare who's making the effort, but *you* – you're struggling to put your ideas down, whereas he managed it rather well several centuries ago.

So search ruthlessly for such padding. Happily, it's fairly easy to spot, even early on; and once you've trained yourself to seek it out and get rid of it, you should find that after a while it drops away from your style quite naturally.

2. Dead expressions II: clichés

One could devote a whole book to this subject; indeed, many have. All I can do, or want to do, in this brief section is to get you to be fiercely on the look-out in your style for expressions that have been around too long and used too often to retain any currency at all. There are literally thousands of examples, from which I offer you these few – on the basis that they always make me cringe:

Achilles' heel; acid test; thin end of the wedge; cart before the horse; letting his heart rule his head; moment of truth; melting-pot; everything at sixes and sevens; like looking for a needle in a haystack; nose to the grindstone; toe the line; ring the changes; head-over-heels in love; cat among the pigeons; nigger in the woodpile

and so on. Even if you don't actively dislike these expressions as I do, I hope you can see that they have all become obsolescent through over-use. Even those that once were powerful and even poetic – 'moment of truth', 'needle and haystack', for example – are simply boring now; while others were never very good from the start ('nigger in the woodpile', for instance, has the double disadvantage of being both incomprehensible and offensive) and are yawn-inspiring today.

This is even more true of Proverbs. I suppose they have their uses, though I've always found it hard to see them: the kind of person who quotes a proverb to sum up an individual human experience is the kind of person I'd emigrate to avoid. But on no account should you let them infect your written style. There is almost nothing more dismal than encountering in mid-argument a bromidish phrase like:

> Don't cross your bridges until you come to them/He should have looked before he leapt/Fair words butter no parsnips/Still waters run deep.

The first two are bad enough, but at least they're only boring. I've never found anyone who could give me an adequate explanation of the third, while the fourth is, of course, illiterate – the point about still waters is that they don't run *at all* – that's why they're *still*.

I rather *like* getting annoyed about proverbs, as you may have gathered! But I'm convinced that they have about as legitimate a place in your style as illiteracies like 'ain't', 'could of done', or that modern illiteracy, the all-purpose use of 'situation' (as in 'riot-situation' when you mean 'riot', or, as I read in a recent undergraduate essay, 'Hamlet's eyeball-to-eyeball situation with his mother').

3. Dead words

There will be times when you wish to qualify your statements with an adverb. But don't do it too often: you must trust your material enough to state it plainly at times. So be sparing in your use of these:

> Very; quite; extremely; absolutely; utterly; rather; really; completely; totally.

Save them for times when they're essential. Rid yourself of such flabby expressions as 'very true' (after all, a thing's either true or it isn't – you can't have superlative versions of truth), 'completely and utterly defeated', 'rather wicked', 'quite evil', and so on. Certain words cannot be qualified, and others need it less often than you might think. Once again, too much qualifying creates an impression of timidity as well as padding, and both are damaging to your style.

4. 'Definitely'

I would advise you *never* to use this word. Curiously, rather than *endorsing* a perception, it *undermines* it. If you say something like:

> 'Charles II was definitely a good king'/'Macbeth is definitely a tragic hero'/'Chaucer was definitely a genius'

one somehow gets the impression that the matter is in doubt – as if it's quite possible that Charles II was a *bad* king, Macbeth is neither a hero nor tragic, or that Chaucer was a fourteenth-century hack. Alternatively (or additionally) it suggests childish triumph – 'Yah sucks boo! I've made up my mind about *that*, so there!'. Leave it out: it's hardly ever useful anyway, and looks amateurish.

PS. If you *must* use it, then at least spell it right! It is alarming how many students think it's spelt 'defin*ately*'!

5. Over-use of 'I'

You are writing an essay; *you* know you're writing the essay; the *reader* knows you're writing the essay. So why keep saying 'I think', 'in my opinion', 'it seems to me', 'I find', and so on? It's obvious that the opinions are yours, the thinking, the argument. So in the normal run of things, omit all such unnecessary reminders.

It is especially important to do this because there *are* times when you need to stress that it is your opinion and not another's. If you're making a point that is unusual or controversial, it makes sense to let the reader know that you're aware of its status. 'In my view' is a legitimate opening if you suspect that what follows will not meet with universal agreement; but it's mere irritating padding if it introduces something sound but unremarkable which most readers would accept.

6. Tautology

A tautology is an expression where at least one of the words is redundant. Two obvious, comic examples would be:

> 'a dead corpse'; 'a round circle'.

Most tautologies are more subtle than those, however – and more dangerous to you as a result. O. M. Thomson, in his excellent book, *A*

Matter of Style,* lists a number of common tautologies that he frequently encountered as an examiner: I've italicized the redundancy.

> 'Throughout the *whole* chapter . . .'
> 'The *final* incident with which the chapter ends . . .'
> 'These factors combined *together* to produce . . .'
> 'It was no more than a *mere* passing thought . . .'
> 'But after a while, *however*, he *began to* realize . . .'
> 'He can do no more than *just* follow blindly . . .'

Of course, we all do this in *conversation*; and it can creep into our written style because we are attempting (laudably) to achieve a natural and fluent ease such as we have when talking. But such moments must be watched for: their comic potential undermines your authority, and they also waste time.

7. Organization: paragraphs and sentence-length

I'm surprised by how many able students reduce the impact of their work by forgetting about such basic things as paragraphs. It is hard to generalize effectively; but I would say that a page of A4 ought to have at least two and probably three paragraphs on average.

There are two good reasons for this. Firstly, if your paragraphs run to over a page, it's almost certain that you're running too many separate points or even arguments into each other, and you need to pause and think out the structure of your material more clearly. And secondly, the consequent absence of any indentation makes the reader's heart sink. His eye notes balefully that it's going to be a long time before it can take a rest; and this can make him quite out-of-sorts with your performance. Too many *short* paragraphs create a sense of scrappiness and superficiality; but too few paragraphs will make your essays very hard work to read, as well as running the risk of getting bogged down.

Sentence-length is a more subtle matter. Ideally, you should vary your sentences. A good snappy sentence is often an excellent tonic to the reader – especially after two or three complex ones. If you include too many short ones, your style will start to resemble a bad parody of Ernest Hemingway; but it's sensible to ensure that the reader has some comfortable moments from time to time. As with all things to do with

* Thomson, O. M. (1973) *A Matter of Style*, Hutchinson, London, pp. 27–29.

style, once you start *thinking* about your sentences properly, a natural and pleasing rhythm should follow fairly soon. At all costs, beware of *rambling* – the kind of sentence that goes on and on, flitting from point to point. A good sentence, however complex, never *loses* the reader: it guides him clearly and confidently over the ground. If you keep that in mind, you should have few problems.

Conclusion

Norman Mailer has written, in what could well be considered a kind of paraphrase of Pascal's remark that heads this Appendix: 'Style is character'.* It takes a long time for people to become fully aware of their own nature; and it also takes a long time to achieve an enviable and natural style. But both processes can be accelerated if you keep aware of yourself. If you just *write*, with no sense of yourself, and with only a vague awareness of which words you're choosing and of how the argument is to progress, your style will almost certainly be by turns awkward, obscure, and flabby. If, however, you trust yourself and are fully alert to the sound and meaning of each phrase you write, you will find that most of the flaws I've discussed will pass you by. Most good students damage their style by trying to take on another 'voice' from their own: they produce phrases not because they *feel* them, but because they imagine they're 'right' or 'weighty'. There's no need to do that. Your mind's done the work; so let your own voice tell us about it.

* Mailer, N. (1967) *Cannibals and Christians*, Deutsch, London, p. 210.

APPENDIX B

● ● ● ● ●

Reading novels and creative literature*

It is, I think, obvious why my six-point programme is unsatisfactory for works of literature. Novels, plays, and poetry cannot be dealt with in this manner – not because there's anything 'holy' about them, but because it simply doesn't work. If you dart through a novel or a Shakespeare play employing the first four 'points' I suggest, you end up precisely where you started, and annoyed to boot. The main reason, of course, is that literary works don't *have* summaries, graphs, illustrations or even chapter headings. And their introductory and concluding sections work in a different, less straightforward, way.

So how can you increase your rate of coverage if the central part of your course is literature? To come to terms with a major play takes a lot of time. Even more arduous is a text the length of *Jane Eyre* or *Our Mutual Friend* (both frequent choices for 'A'-level and undergraduate courses). When you remember that reading the text is only the first stage – you've then got to discuss, analyse and absorb it – the task can seem forbidding.

One answer is to cultivate 'skip-reading', which I've looked at already. This provides useful 'ignition', which is important; but, clearly, it won't do much *more* than get you started, especially if you're missing out twenty pages at a time. By all means use it to kick you off; but you need something else as well.

Letting the book do the work

I haven't yet mentioned the simplest kind of 'speed-reading' of all – that of reading the book very fast, without pausing to mull anything over, and not being at all concerned at the bits that make no sense or seem dull.

* This section is primarily meant for students specializing in Literature.

I have found this method consistently valuable ever since I started 'A' levels twenty years ago. When I read in this way, I don't *consciously* ignore anything, as I would if 'skip-reading'. This method is more passive. I make no decisions, no choices, no clever short-cuts. I let the *book* do the work, not me – I let it wash over me, leaving the book to determine which bits 'stick'.

Let me give an example. My favourite novel is *Anna Karenina* – hardly an original judgement, as most lovers of literature would consider it among the greatest works ever written. One of its major features is its length – over 850 pages in my Penguin edition. It is doubly daunting to pick up such a tome knowing it to be not only very long but also one of the greatest aesthetic achievements of all time. How, one asks oneself, am I going even to *begin* to cope with something like this?

When I first read the novel at the age of seventeen, I covered it in two days. I positively *belted* through it, determined to get to the end as quickly as I could. This was not because I disliked it – quite the reverse. I was hoping to acquire, as fast as possible, a *sense* of its majesty, and a kind of 'skeletal' idea of its plot, style and characters. And I believe I achieved this. I had an at least basic knowledge of the plot (or, rather, the *plots*), and some sense of how these separate narrative strands were interwoven. I knew something about all the major characters; and I had an awed awareness of the grandeur of the writing. I could see, however vaguely, that Tolstoy was equally masterly whether describing the subtlest emotions, the most vigorous physical activities, or the feel of the ever-changing landscape. In short, I knew something of what the book was about, and a little bit about why it has such a reputation.

I've read *Anna Karenina* probably twenty times since then. I still don't feel I 'know' it really well, and I imagine I won't feel that even when I've read it a further twenty times – it's that kind of book. And that is very much the point. As I said at the start of this chapter, *any* significant work of literature (and it's unlikely you'll be asked to centre your studies on anything less) has a richness and variety that will continue to yield new pleasures on the tenth, twentieth or umpteenth reading; and nobody will expect you to plumb *all* its depths in a mere two or three years. With this in mind, a tearaway first reading is perfectly sensible, and will very probably encourage you to make an early and more sober return to the text. The alternative – plodding haltingly through it over a period of weeks – is unlikely to be more efficient in terms of retention. Your response will be less vibrant if you plod, and you may end up hoping to God you never have to open the book again. Not a very productive attitude for a student faced with a set text.

Think of a novel as a painting or a piece of music

When we first look at a painting, we take in a general, over-all impression. We note the subject, the colour, the size, the 'feeling' it radiates. Later, returning to it, we start to notice details: the *blending* and *number* of colours, the way the eye is drawn this way and that by the picture's *line*, the perspective, and other subtler things. Still later, we may see evidence of particular techniques, acquire a full sense of the picture's structure, and be able to say with some authority and analytic prowess what the picture *does* and why it is impressive.

Similarly with a piece of music. At first we will merely be aware of tunes, the instruments used, and the 'atmosphere' engendered. Subsequently, we will start to realize how the tunes relate to each other, precisely how the composer deploys the various instruments and why, and how he uses dynamics and even silence. Eventually, our appreciation will grow to include grasp of structure, and a familiarity with its themes/tunes that makes proper sense of individual phrases.

A novel can be approached in much the same way. First time round, you will get an over-all sense of its structure and subject, plus a general idea of its style, pace, and characters. Just as the painting and the music are not *studied* in detail at first, so should you 'glance' at your novel, establishing a pleasant, undemanding acquaintance. The study comes later – when you're in shape for it.

Works of art are complex, profoundly intricate things. No-one can understand them quickly, however clever they may be. The person who expects to achieve adequate mastery through one laborious 'go' at a novel not only understands nothing about how literature works: he knows very little about how his own mind operates. By now I hope you are not such a person! So read as fast and as 'superficially' as you like: the detailed digging that has to be done later will be all the easier and more successful as a result.

APPENDIX C

● ● ● ● ●

Some simple relaxation and fitness exercises

There are few things more maddening than being cheerily told 'Relax!' when you're feeling like an over-wound watch-spring. It usually seems about as sensible and tactful as telling someone who's depressed to 'cheer up!'. Nevertheless, there are ways in which you can reduce *physical* tension at least; and that can often ease the mind's jangling as well. So here's a simple routine that you will find calms you down quite effectively and pleasantly:

(1) Lie down on your back, or sit in a chair which fully supports your back.

(2) Close your eyes.

(3) Think about your head. Feel the forehead-muscles relaxing. Relax your eyelids, and let your jaw go slack. Let your tongue fall to the bottom of your mouth. Start to take deep breaths.

(4) Now move down to your shoulders. Let them go loose, and allow your arms to go limp.

(5) Relax your neck: let your head roll gently until you find an agreeable position.

(6) Let your stomach go slack. It is probably the tensest part of you at such times, so take your time. Concentrate on smoothing away all the creases that seem to line it inside.

(7) Tense and relax your right arm, several times. Then tense it once more, and *slowly* relax it from the top of the shoulder to the finger-tips.

(8) Do the same with your left arm.

(9) Tense and relax your right leg several times. Then tense it once more, and slowly let the tension go, from hip down to toes.

(10) Do the same with your left leg.

(11) Now listen to any sound from within your body – heartbeat,

breathing, stomach. Pick one such sound and focus on it. Block out all other sounds and thoughts.

(12) Tense and relax your whole body, at five-second intervals. Do this twice more. Then, slowly open your eyes and sit upright. Take a long slow 'stretch'.

You can even use these at an exam desk, and certainly anywhere else. They soften tension through being physically pleasant; and for a valuable five minutes they reduce all that mental 'buzzing' – or at least reduce your anxious concentration on it.

Everyday fitness exercises are also good for sharpening your muscle-tone and general alertness. If in doubt about your physical state, consult your doctor first; but I wouldn't imagine these will over-tax many of you:

(1) Toe touching. With feet apart; then with feet together. You can also try touching each foot with the opposite hand. Keep your legs straight, or as straight as you can bear!

(2) Press-ups. Excellent for toning you up and controlling the breathing. Women sometimes find these hard, and should be prepared to improvise.

(3) Sit-ups. Lie on your back, and if possible hook your toes under something solid (i.e. unlikely to move). Clasp your hands behind your neck; and then haul yourself up to a sitting position. Real masochists can try to bring their head down to meet their knees! Repeat 5–10 times, or until the stomach muscles lodge a formal protest!

(4) 'Cycling.' Lie on your back; raise your legs about 2 feet; then 'pedal' as smoothly as you can. Regulate pace according to taste/pain level.

(5) The straight leg-lift. Lie on your back, legs together. Raise them six inches. Hold that position for 5 seconds. Lower. Repeat 5 times. Then repeat, but, after raising, splay each leg to the side, maintaining a 6-in distance off the ground. Do this three times, then return to together-position and lower.

Of course, if you're keen to get truly fit in a more athletic sense, these would qualify only as warm-up exercises. But for the less vigorous, they will keep your body quite freshly tuned on about fifteen minutes a day. And the better you feel physically, the more alert and 'bright' you will be in your study.

● ● ● ● ●

Bibliography

There are now a great many 'study aids' of various kinds. One cannot hope to list them all; and to be frank I wouldn't want to do so: the titles listed are those I have myself found helpful, and would recommend to any student.

General

Buzan, T. (1974) *Use Your Head*, BBC, London.
de Bono, E. (1982) *de Bono's Thinking Course*, BBC, London.
Freeman, R. (1982) *Mastering Study Skills*, Macmillan, London.
Gibbs, G. (1981) *Teaching Students To Learn*, Open University, Milton Keynes.
Russell, P. (1979) *The Brain Book*, RKP, London.

Memory

Baddeley, D. (1976) *The Psychology of Memory*, Basic Books, London.
Baddeley, D. (1983) *Your Memory: A User's Guide*, Penguin, Harmondsworth.
Yates, Frances A. (1969) *The Art of Memory*, Penguin, Harmondsworth.

Writing

Collinson, D. J. (1982) *Writing English*: A workbook for students, Pan, London.
Lewis, R. (1979) *How To Write Essays*, Macmillan, London.
Thomson, O. M. (1973) *A Matter of Style*, Hutchinson, London.
Turk, C. (1979) *Effective Writing*, Spon, London.

Reading

de Leeuw, M. and E. (1965) *Read Better, Read Faster*, Penguin, Harmondsworth.
Moore, J. (1980) *Reading and Thinking in English*, Oxford University Press, Oxford.

Grammar and basics

Carey, G. V. (1971) *Mind The Stop*, Penguin, Harmondsworth.
Gowers, E. (1962) *The Complete Plain Words*, Penguin, Harmondsworth.
Thomson, O. M. (1973) *Essential Grammar*, OUP, Oxford.

Research papers and graduate work

Watson, G. (1970) *The Literary Thesis*, Longman, Harlow.
Winkler, A. C. and McCuen, J. R. (1979) *Writing the Research Paper*, Harcourt Brace, New York.

Pamphlets

I would like enthusiastically to commend two pamphlets that should still be available:

Bowles, J. H. (1981) *How To Study*. From the Author, Bagmere Bank Cottage, Brereton, Sandbach, Cheshire.
Chibnall, B. (1979) *Study Skills for Sixth Forms*. From the Media Service Unit, University of Sussex, Falmer, Brighton.

Index